Fit For Business: [illegible] To Deal With Stress & Create A Healthy Work Life Balance

Andrew Bridgewater

Published By: AndrewBridgewater.com

Email : Andrew@AndrewBridgewater.com

First Edition published 2014
Second Edition published 2016

ISBN: 978-0-9955259-0-0

The information contained in this book is for education and personal development purposes only. It is not produced or recommended as a way of diagnosing or treating an illness or condition. Please consult your medical practitioner qualified in treating that condition. The publisher and author of this book do not provide medical advice, nor do they prescribe any remedies or assume any responsibility for those choosing to treat themselves. Please consult with your Doctor before commencing any program of exercise.

About The Author

Andrew Bridgewater is a Chartered Psychologist and MBA who specialises in helping leaders and managers respond to stress in highly effective, healthy and sustainable ways which positively impact the bottom line of the business.

His other products include:

Fit For Business – an 8 week audio home study course which includes a 1:1 coaching session
www.AndrewBridgewater.com/fitforbusiness-coaching

The Alkaline Diet Success Formula – a 6 week audio home study course, including interviews with other health experts from around the world
www.TheAkalineDietExperts.com/6-weeks-to-a-new-you

To enquire about booking Andrew as a speaker or to request a 1:1 consultation, please visit
www.AndrewBridgewater.com or email
Andrew@AndrewBridgewater.com

To connect with Andrew via social media :-
www.Facebook.com/FitForBusiness
www.YouTube.com/TheAndrewBridgewater
www.UK.LinkedIn.com/in/AndrewBridgewater/
www.Twitter.com/AddVitality

Table Of Contents

Introduction

This is a book for business leaders who are at "the point of willingness" and ready to make some simple but powerful lifestyle changes with encouragement and practical support.

Back in 2006, I experienced what in the old days would have been referred to as a "nervous breakdown". Those seem like a very loaded two words when I look at them now. I'm pleased to say that ten years on, I have never felt better in my life and know for sure that the dark days are well behind me. As a Chartered Psychologist I've learned far more from my own life experience about how to deal with stress and create a healthy work life balance than I ever did from studying or taking exams. I wrote this book to help others who may be experiencing what I often felt until I discovered the ideas I'm about to share.

Did you really set out in business to feel this stressed and tired?

Are you finding it difficult to get life and work into any sort of balance?

Are relationships with friends and family suffering?

Are you battling with low levels of energy and libido?

Are you unhappy with your body image and what that's saying to others?

Are you struggling with health challenges that are sucking the lifeblood out of you?

Do you want some help to move your whole life forward?

The principles and simple steps set out here have been derived from my own life experience, some of it highly painful and difficult to endure. However, I have a firmly held belief that "everything in life happens for a reason" and that the reason I experienced such tough times was to share the recovery and health success formula with the world, so helping others avoid going through the same pain. The experience cost me dearly and I don't want you to have to pay this sort of price. The end of a 20 year marriage, separation from my 2 sons as well as the humiliation and embarrassment of being admitted to hospital with stress-induced depression.

I've also written the book to help redress the social stigma of experiencing severe stress, something that caused me to remain highly secretive until now about some powerful life lessons that will benefit others in very significant ways. I now feel a duty to share these lessons with the world.

This material in this book is practical and personal - it's not a set of ideas written by an academic psychologist.

Looking after your health is vitally important and crucial for business success. When I began to experience severe stress back in 2006, I realised that there is very little practical advice and support available. This book will give you tools and techniques to mitigate the risk of experiencing health problems brought on by stressful life circumstances and help you develop a healthy work life balance. None of us can anticipate the many challenges that life brings, ranging from bereavement to loss of a meaningful relationship or livelihood. What we can do however, is put some simple habits in place to enable us to deal with whatever life throw at us – in or outside business. This is a very reassuring position to be in – knowing that whatever happens, you'll be able to handle it!

The aim of this book is to help you understand and condition a simple set of healthy habits to deal with stress and create balance for life, without ever having to rely on pills or therapy if the going gets really tough. These habits are all "easy to do and easy not to do". In other words, if you don't do one of them today, you probably won't notice the difference tomorrow or the day after. It's the daily compounding of these simple habits that creates a massive wave of change over a period of just a few weeks. This is the philosophy of the slight edge, set out by Jeff Olson in his book "The Slight Edge: Secret To a Successful Life". The book can be summed up in a single sentence...small simple things compound to produce a massive difference, but you have to do them to benefit.

It might help to know that if you are in the midst of some tough life circumstances right now that I genuinely understand and have felt your pain. I've overcome major problems with stress and a life out of balance and this book shares my philosophy and formula for lifelong health, energy and wellbeing. However, the aim isn't just to help you avoid burnout, but to begin to thrive on stress and use it as a powerful force for good in your own and others' lives.

By applying what is shared here, you'll experience a host of benefits going well beyond business. You'll get more done in less time, cut through problems with ease, be more fun to be with inside and outside work, sleep better, suffer much less in the way of common ailments such as colds, flu, stomach upsets, headaches, skin problems, aches and pains. You'll also reduce the risk of contracting a major illness and old age needn't be a process of decrepit decline – you really can enjoy great health and energy into your 80s and beyond. I know this sounds like an impressive list of benefits, but it's just a start! You don't have to believe a word; just put the simple health ideas I'm about to share into practice and then experience the benefits in your mind and body.

Writing this book feels nothing less profound than fulfilling three key reasons for my existence :-

1. To pass on to others the huge learning I have experienced through the adversity of a major stress-related illness.

2. To redress the stigma of stress-related illness as something that a person does not just recover from but which can actually lead them to become stronger. This is a crucial point in dealing with a social stigma which can regard people who've had a problem in the past as somehow damaged and weakened.

3. To be able to share a simple formula for lifelong physical and mental wellbeing that creates results which are nothing short of miraculous. Let's start the journey together right away.

Chapter 1 - Why This Stuff Matters: A Personal Perspective

"The further down and out you have been, the further up and in you can go"
Dr John Demartini

Dark Night Of The Soul

Lying on hard hospital bed in May 2006, I seriously wondered if my life was over. I was surrounded by some very ill people and was in the midst of what I subsequently came to understand as psychotic depression, a severe form of the condition which results in the sufferer losing touch with reality and imagining all manner of sights, sounds and smells. The best way to describe it is as a waking nightmare which went on for several weeks. Before I was admitted, my meager and hastily packed bag of personal possessions was searched for anything I could possibly use to injure or kill myself. Just as well because I would not have hesitated given the chance. I was admitted to hospital for my own safety and unless I had agreed to be admitted voluntarily, I would have been taken in compulsorily.

How The Stress Built Up To Breaking Point

The story I'm about to share is highly personal, but I feel it needs to be told so as to help others avoid the same problems in future. By 2004, I was 43 years old and had almost qualified as a Chartered Psychologist, although the learning that was to take place over the next 2 years was far more profound than anything gained from studying for an OU Diploma in Psychology and a Master's degree at Bristol University. I had been married for 15 years and had two sons aged 8 and 6. I lived as part of a "normal" family unit and we holidayed once a year and both worked hard. Looking back now, I felt a sense of emptiness, a lack of fulfillment and began casting around to try to fill the imaginary void.

During 10 months of 2004 spent capital fundraising for the construction of a new theatre in Leicester, I met some very successful and influential entrepreneurs. The legacy of that time was that I wanted to create a massive break-through in my business and especially to experience higher levels of financial success. My wife, Sue had started running a course for football managers at the university where she worked as a senior lecturer and was coming into contact with some very wealthy and successful people too. Liking what she saw there, I felt slightly inadequate and decided to take some steps to significantly improve our financial position, not that it was bad at that point. Still in New Year resolution mode in January 2005, my brother and I met up one evening at a pub mid-way between where we both lived. Over a few pints of beer, we decided that this was to be the year that things changed for us both. Ideas started being thrown around and Peter and I agreed to come up with some specific plans to create a business together.

Everything starts with an idea. Peter mentioned that Cyprus seemed to be a booming economy in early 2005 and that he knew some people who were looking at investing in property over there. Sue and I had been to Cyprus for a holiday in 1998 just before Sam was born but I knew little about the island as a place to invest or do business. I signed up for a weekend course in property investing with a company called "Beware The Sharks". How that name rings true now with what was subsequently to happen in Cyprus.

As with any course of that type, there were "upsells" and opportunities to take things further. I decided to travel to

Cyprus on a long weekend inspection visit with a sister company of "Beware The Sharks" called "Invest In Cyprus". Peter came along too and we spent 4 days viewing properties in southern Cyprus, together with a small coach load of other potential investors. During the visit, I agreed to purchase a 2-bedroom villa in Perivolia which was due to be built in the next 6 months. I didn't sleep a wink the night I'd agreed to buy the house. Peter meanwhile wasn't too inspired by Cyprus and decided not to make an investment. How wise I thought, not long afterwards.

Ultimately, the purchase of the property in Perivolia fell through and interestingly, 10 years later, that particular property remained unsold. I did however visit Larnaca again and decided to buy a less expensive property which I felt would be suitable for long term rental or holiday lets. This particular house comprised 4 walls and a roof when I first viewed the site in July 2005. This time, I followed through with the purchase and Sue and I became the proud owners of a rental property in Cyprus. At least that's how it felt for a few months.

I felt that I was on a roll and 2005 became the year of "personal development" seminars for me. As well as the weekend property seminar in February, I went to Tony Robbins' "Unleash The Power Within" in May, a 1 week neuro linguistic programing course in September and Harv Eker's "Millionaire Mind Intensive" in New Jersey USA and was there for my 44th birthday in early December. With the benefit of hindsight, it was all too much and my limiting beliefs around success at that time couldn't adapt to the information that my mind was being fed. Consequently, I began to subconsciously sabotage any success I was beginning to experience at that time. I'll talk more about the power of beliefs later and how crucial they are in every aspect of our lives, especially in business.

The first warning signs of what was to come occurred whilst I was in New Jersey for Harv Eker's seminar. I began to have negative thoughts about the purchase of the house in Cyprus and started having difficulty getting off to sleep, waking early feeling tired. Sue and I had committed to a large mortgage to fund the purchase and it began not to seem like such a great idea after all. "Buyer's remorse" on a massive scale is one description of what I started to experience and something which ultimately turned into all-out depression 3 months later. It's kind of difficult taking a house back to the place you bought it, clutching the receipt and asking for your money to be returned.

You might think that ending up in hospital with chronic depression was a dramatic overreaction and it does look like that to me now after what I've handled since. The beginning of a prolonged and very negative period of thinking started just before Christmas 2005 when for some reason, I decided to check the price of unsold properties on the same development where Sue and I had purchased near Larnaca. The property market in southern Cyprus had begun to crash by this point and I discovered that equivalent properties to the one we had purchased were available for around 25% less – and this price fall was in less than 6 months. It was a real shock and I didn't know how to break the news to my wife, so I didn't - for over a month.

By the time I confessed to Sue that this first stepping stone to financial freedom was turning into a miserable wet walk in a quagmire, I had begun to sleep very badly and was feeling extremely stressed. It seemed that I was spending every moment of the waking day and night reflecting on the foolish decision I had made, one which I felt had the potential to cause serious financial harm to my family. Sue's reaction to the news of the property price fall was nothing other than totally supportive but I still felt like a total fool and a failure. By focusing on the problem for the next 3 months, as opposed to the solution, I ended up in hospital. Not hard to do with 4 months of literally non-stop negative thinking under my belt. Buying an overseas property for the first time, taking a large mortgage to do so and then seeing the price fall through the floor within a few months was much more than I could handle at the time. Everyone including me was expecting the property market in Cyprus to keep rising as the introduction of the Euro moved nearer and money flooded into the country from countries such as Russia. But the market crashed spectacularly, not just in Cyprus but in other countries including Spain and Portugal.

Something I have subsequently realised is that no "thing" can ever really make you happy in life. The property portfolio, the place in the sun that many dreamed of and almost as many made a reality; none of this is a prescription for happiness and can even become a potent one for unhappiness, as in my case.

The whole experience also taught me that the power of thought is immense and that we really do become what we think about. Easy to read in a book but so much more powerful to experience. I subsequently realised that if 4 months of negative thinking could bring me literally to death's door, then surely a lifetime of positive thinking afterwards could have an impact too. It feels like a huge privilege to be able to pass on to you the profound lessons I've learned.

It's Not What Happens But What You Do With What Happens

The summer of 2006 was spent rehabilitating in the world outside hospital. I had been placed on high doses of medication for depression whilst there and these continued under the supervision of an outpatient psychiatrist. One side effect of the medication was that, as I was told to expect, I put on an inordinate amount of weight which isn't exactly great for creating a positive mood. At the time, it seemed there was nothing I could do about the weight gain. I subsequently found out that the medication impacted my appetite. Perhaps it was actually better that I was alive and fat than dead.

As a way of doing something constructive and to get out of the house, I applied for a job stacking shelves and serving behind the counter at my local Co-op supermarket. At the interview, I told the area manager that I was applying for the job as part of my rehabilitation from depression and he was wonderfully supportive. It was clearly unusual for someone aged 45 with 2 masters degrees to apply for work at £6 an hour. I spent over a month there and began to feel massively better. So much so that I applied for a job with a firm of business psychologists in Oxford and was offered a job towards the end of July. This was huge progress, given that I'd only been released from hospital on 19th May. The medication was working and had given me the breathing space to put life back on track. This is the only reason I can think of to take medication which has such massive side effects; to enable the patient to begin to deal with the underlying causes of their depression or anxiety whilst the drugs are busy masking the symptoms.

Before I went into hospital, Sue had moved out of our bedroom into a spare room because I was sleeping so badly. It turned out that she never moved back into the marital bedroom and I found this particularly difficult to deal with. We were never to sleep together again. I think my wife found it hard to trust me and to some extent went along with the stigma of mental illness; that I was now damaged goods and would in some way always be vulnerable to an outbreak of stress-induced depression or anxiety. Infact nothing could be further from the truth and one of the reasons I need to write this book is to redress this aspect of the social stigma of mental illness. Some people manifest stress through a physical illness and some through mental illness; each person has their own "crack of least resistance". I have always enjoyed robust physical health, even when I was seriously depressed. Tragically I can remember thinking "why can't my body just give up and put me out of this abject misery"?

I found and started a new job in Oxford on 3rd September 2006 and soon found myself immersed in the world of corporate training. Apart from gaining about 2 stone in weight in as many months, I felt alright and able to tackle the challenges of a very demanding and stressful job. The fact that I was employed for the first time in 11 years would I hope, give Sue some confidence and help to repair our shattered marriage. I still loved my wife and wanted nothing more at that time than to mend our relationship and move forward together. However, it was not to be and the next year was spent with me working away from home, putting on even more weight while staying in hotels, eating too much and not getting enough exercise. One of the real challenges having put on around 50 lbs or 22 kilos was that I couldn't even run for a bus, let along contemplate a jog or cycle as I'd always done before. So I found myself in a vicious circle from which it felt very hard to escape.

The outpatient psychiatrist was very determined to keep me on medication for at least 2 years but I had other ideas. No one really knows the long term side effects of anti-depressant medication. All I knew was that I was becoming very fat and that my libido had packed its bags and departed long ago, which was probably just as well, otherwise I might have been tempted to have an affair.

I can recall the precise moment when beliefs I held about my weight and body image started to shift. Feeling overweight, tired and old, well beyond my 45 years, I got into a lift in a hotel in London at the end of a busy day of training in June 2007. The lift had a 4-way mirror, one mirror on each wall and I caught a view of myself that I'd not seen before. Looking tired, stressed and very overweight, I made a committed decision at that point. All it takes to change our lives is a true decision (meaning to cut oneself off from any other possibility). I decided there and then to get healthy, lose the weight and dump the stress and depression for good. Within 6 months, I had lost 3.5 stone (50 lbs or 22kilos) and was feeling better than I had done since my mid-20s. The formula I used to deal with stress and lose the weight was shared in an eBook I wrote a year later entitled The AV Diet (add vitality) and I'll share all that and more with you in the subsequent chapters of this book. It all began with a decision. The image I saw in the lift that day was powerful enough to blow away any limiting beliefs I had about being able to get healthy in order to lose weight permanently. More than that, the way I lost the weight turned out to be a profound and natural anti-depressant formula too.

Despite my worries, Sue and I were able to hold onto the property in Cyprus and continue to pay the mortgage. In February 2008, I went over there on my own for a long weekend with the intention of putting the property up for sale. The day after I came back, I asked Sue what she thought we should do with the house in Cyprus. Sue replied "Do what you like, it will all come out in the divorce anyway" or words to that effect. I was devastated. It was the first time either of us had mentioned the D word, although it had been "the elephant in the room" for some considerable time.

Immediately Sue had said those words, I took off on my bike into the countryside taking the mobile phone with me and called my brother, my mum and my dad. It was the conversation every impending divorcee dreads having with their family. "It's all over between Sue and I, we're getting a divorce" I said, letting go of the tears. Suddenly I felt very alone, more than I'd felt since being in hospital. Now I was going to lose my wife and be separated from my two wonderful sons.

If it hadn't been for my job and some wonderful friends and

colleagues at the company in Oxford, the next few weeks in March 2008 would have been unbearable. As it was, I managed and reflected that I'd already been through far worse. Perhaps Sue had waited until she felt I was strong enough to cope before announcing that she wanted a divorce. I even searched the internet and read an eBook called "How To Stop Your Divorce" but that didn't work. So here I was again, seemingly at the bottom. But something was different this time. I knew I'd be alright because I'd already been to hell and back. Once you become a graduate of the University Of Rock Bottom, nothing else is the same again. There's a resilience which goes beyond any reserves I might have previously possessed and it's important to be able to bottle and share that resilience formula for the benefit of others. This is what I'm seeking to do in this book.

I started seeing Lynn, a family friend, a few months after Sue had dropped the D word bombshell and enlivened by what I thought at the time was a wonderful new relationship, began to give some thought to where my career was going. By this time, I'd spent almost 2 years with the company in Oxford and was financially and emotionally back on track. I had slowly come off anti-depressant medication in September 2007 and replaced it with a combination of fish oil and evening primrose oil, which seemed just as effective, if not more so and with no nasty side effects. I felt strong and capable of venturing back out of the employed world again.

In early July 2008, I received an email from Mark Anastasi whom I met at the NLP certification course in London nearly 3 years earlier. Mark was offering 3 individuals the opportunity to be coached by him personally to establish an internet-based business. This seemed the opportunity I was looking for and I willingly paid my £2997. For the next few months, I wrote The AV Diet, my first eBook by getting up an hour earlier and writing before beginning my training day with the company in

Oxford. The eBook was finished in about 6 weeks.

Somehow I thought that by creating an information product and a web sales page, I would be able to quit my job and enjoy “the laptop lifestyle”. I resigned from the job in Oxford and left in early October 2008, continuing to do some work as an associate until Christmas that year when the recession started to hit and the company started to feel the pinch quite badly.

Understandably, Lynn was uncomfortable with the risk I was taking in giving up the job to focus on creating an internet business. I was determined to make a success of it and ploughed on, creating a series of websites targeting different niches including middle aged men, mothers seeking to lose the baby weight and the alkaline diet. I spent tens of thousands of pounds on coaching, website development and other business set up costs. I found a way to make a loan from my pension fund to cover the business start up costs, figuring that the best pension investment I could make would be in my own startup business and skills. This was different to being a management consultant and involved learning a whole new business model. There are a plethora of “experts” out there willing to take substantial amounts of money in return for business startup coaching and other programmes. I paid them handsomely in the belief that it was a powerful short circuit to success only to find that there is really no fast track.

Unfortunately, the biggest challenge was still waiting around the corner. In July 2009, Mark Anastasi introduced me to Jarl Moe. Mark said he had invested money and was receiving a return of around 6% a month on his money through trading on the foreign exchange markets. Jarl Moe seemed to be running a legitimate operation in Cyprus and is a very confident smooth talker. In August 2009, I sent approximately £20,000 to Jarl Moe’s operation. This was money I had saved to pay for my sons’ education. The website which tracked investment performance indicated that returns were around 3% a month. This was considerably less than Mark Anastasi had reported but I wasn't unduly concerned. People were withdrawing money without problems, although I decided to let mine compound for higher growth. In the subsequent 12 months, I sent another £30,000 confident that my money was being well invested in a niche opportunity which was not available by invitation only and not open to the public.

Whilst in Cyprus I met up with Jarl Moe's office manager, Lin Crawford who administered his operation. This lady went out of her way to be extremely friendly and introduced me to some of her own friends in an attempt to win my trust and confidence. So much so, that I parted with £80,000 of my pension fund believing that I was investing in organic cotton and forex trading directly.

Cutting a long story short, all seemed to be well until I requested a withdrawal of Euro 5000 to pay for my sons' school fees in May 2012. Over 4 years later, I am still awaiting that money and have received no return on either the £50,000 forex investment or the £80,000 pension fund investments. Jarl Moe was arrested on suspicion of committing fraud by police in central London in May 2013 and held for 24 hours before being released on police bail. It seems that hundreds of other people were also taken in by him and that he has operated a classic "ponzi scheme" where profits are paid to initial investors from the funds paid in by later investors. It's a well worked scam. My response to the problems I've experienced has been to focus on the solution and I have worked very hard to find the money for school fees which I had been relying on from the proceeds of the investment with Jarl Moe.

After my experiences in 2006, this was a far bigger challenge over a much more protracted period of time and the problem remains unresolved to this day. Somehow, I have managed to keep the boys at the same school and yet each time I write out a very large cheque at the start of term, I'm reminded of the money I had invested with Jarl Moe and it still hurts a great deal. However, what the experience has proved beyond all doubt is that I am far stronger mentally and psychologically than at any time in my life. I have learned to cope with levels of stress and uncertainty that would have totally floored me 10 years ago.

I also feel that I have busted the myth that a severe episode of stress-induced illness makes a person prone to further episodes in future. Rather like happens with a broken bone, I feel stronger for the break and better able to handle whatever comes up in future. Anyone can experience major stressors at any time in life and I have learned from first principles that it's not what happens to us but what we do with what happens that ultimately makes the difference.

This is the success formula that I want to pass on to you in this book. I hope it can be as life changing for you as it has been for me.

Since publishing the first edition in 2014, I have taken a full time job and experienced many more stress and work life balance challenges inherent in the corporate world. This allows me to update the book and write as someone who can more fully identify with the lives of senior level employees with highly demanding jobs. I've been able to fully road test all the concepts and principles I wrote about in 2014 and my stress levels have been totally manageable and work life balanced in a very tough and rapidly changing role. I came back to Cyprus for 6 days to begin the process of updating and adding to the book – a very fitting place to do it.

Chapter 2 - Fit For Business In 12 Weeks

The 12 Week Challenge

Following the 12 week challenge is your quickest way to deal with stress and get work and life into balance. Just use the information in this section for 12 weeks. Then judge the usefulness of the information by experiencing amazing results in your body, mind, work and whole life.

It's not essential to stop doing, eating or drinking everything you have grown to like. Just begin with some simple changes and watch the results (expect others to notice too) The beauty of the approach that I'm about to share with you is that it involves getting healthy in order to be significantly more energetic and productive in business. It's not necessary to become an outcast from colleagues and clients or deny yourself anything. Quite the opposite.

My approach to living with abundant health and managing stress is revolutionary and exciting. It doesn't require a calorie control diet, patches, pills or surgery. Neither is it a fad; I just want to help you make some small, simple and slightly different lifestyle choices. The small daily changes compounded over 12 weeks will lead to a massive difference. And that's really all I'm talking about – small, simple slight edge changes made every day. Easy to do, easy not to do.

The beauty of the Fit For Business formula that I'm about to share with you is that it's really simple and it works – provided you use and act on the information. The approach works on the basis that the best way to live with energy, low stress and balance permanently is to get healthy first and then stay healthy. After all, what else do you really have? Getting healthy and energetic will benefit you and your business and you might even pass on some great habits to colleagues, friends and loved ones. If Richard Branson says that the best thing that he does for his business is work out regularly, it's worth taking notice and we'll be going much further than just working out over the next 12 weeks together.

It's easy to be so busy juggling all the priorities in your hectic life and forget about your most valued possession, your health. Getting to and maintaining a healthy lifestyle is something few business people stumble across by accident, but the benefits are enormous and include:-

- Dramatically reducing the incidence of illness (both minor and major) That's a massive boost to the bottom line!
- Feeling great virtually all of the time, rather than every now and again or when it's a beautiful day outside
- Greater mental clarity, more effective problem solving and a much higher tolerance of stress
- Getting more done in the same amount of time because you have so much more energy
- Becoming a more confident person, therefore attracting the opportunities that will take you and your business where you want to go, much faster

How To Use Fit For Business In 12 Weeks

Read and most importantly, apply a section of the program each week. Don't overload yourself by trying to follow all the ideas at once. As you listen, do remember to follow up the links I refer to and most importantly, *act on the information.* Remember that as the ancient Buddhist saying goes "To know and not to do is not yet to know".

You are what you think, drink and eat because every cell in your body regenerates within a 2-year period. At the start of your program in particular, it really helps to remember this. It also helps to bear in mind that whereas some simple daily discipline weighs ounces, a lifetime of regret weighs tons. With a little commitment (and I'll show you how to get this), what you have embarked on here will add up to a massive change for the better. You'll never want to go back to that old toxic, high-stress lifestyle again.

Before we start, just a word or two about measurement. As you start "Fit For Business", it's useful to measure your resting heart rate as well as the size of your waist, thighs, upper arms and neck. There will be times when you weigh yourself and don't seem to have lost any pounds. Your body chemistry and body shape will be changing so instead of weighing yourself, check and see if you have lost inches from the above places instead. So I strongly suggest putting the scales away for the first 6 weeks of the program, focusing instead on how your body feels and how your clothes fit.

Any effective health and wellness program must be based on learning how to change lifestyle habits. Re-learning old-established habits is the cornerstone of any effective program and is the only way to become permanently fit and healthy. This way, you change for good and don't succumb to a lifetime pattern of yo-yo dieting and variable health. Most "diets" don't work because they don't focus on conditioning new habits or patterns for life. Many business people just like you have followed the formula I'm about to share with you and it works. Do the same and *I promise that it will work for you.* Let's make a start.

Week 1 - Winning The Mental Game Of Health In Business

Motivation is a key factor in the success or failure of any lifestyle change. Why do people join gyms and health clubs in January and often cancel their memberships by March? Without compelling goals and clear motivators, it can be very difficult to stick to any new lifestyle plan for more than a couple of weeks or so.

Life has a habit of getting in the way doesn't it? That family weekend away with friends, trips to McDonalds with the children, the biscuits and cakes on offer at seminars. The list goes on…and that's just the food component.

How do you stay on track amidst all this? The answer is clear and specific goals, coupled with explicit reasons (motives) for wanting to get healthy in the first place.

If you're overweight for example, start by making a truly committed decision to lose a specific amount of weight and keep it off for life. A decision means a clear sense of certainly and cutting yourself off from any other possibility. If you're not sure what certainty feels like for you, think for a moment about whether the sun will come up tomorrow. How do you know it will and are you certain? Where is the feeling in your body and how do you experience certainly? That's exactly how you can feel now.

Let's think about clear goals and compelling sources of motivation; a case study might help here. Janet is a business owner, approaching 35 and when she came to me for coaching, weighed 12 stone or just under 170lbs. Janet is 5ft 6ins tall and her goal was to lose 25lbs, most of it around her middle in 6 months and keep the weight off. This is a very achievable objective with some simple changes to daily lifestyle.

At the start of Janet's program, we talked through some specific reasons why she wanted to gain energy and lose 25lbs in weight - the following powerful motivators emerged:-
To be able to play tennis on Saturday afternoons again
To be able to run after Jack (her 6 year old) without my back going into spasm
To be able to spend 10 minutes on the children's trampoline without being out of breath
To get back into my size 16 jeans again within a month and my favourite size 12 jeans within 5 months
To not have my children tease me about my belly

These were highly effective and specific motivators for Janet. Notice that one of them is an "away-from" motivator (the last one) while the rest are "towards" motivated.
"Away from" is often a good way to get started with making a change and then it's useful to let some powerful forces pull you towards a new future and keep you motivated when the challenges and distractions arise (as they inevitably do).

The simplest mental conditioning approach is to combine effective goal setting with clear and specific reasons. That's what you're about to do now.

Stop for a moment and note down the reasons you want to gain energy, deal with stress effectively and create a healthy work life balance. If you're driving, please do come back later and do this - list 15 "away from" reasons and 15 "towards" reasons.

"Away From" Reasons – Pain	**"Towards" Reasons - Pleasure**
The painful reasons why I must gain energy, deal with stress effectively and create a healthy work life balance are... (e.g. I no longer..., I am sick and tired of…)	The pleasurable reasons why I must gain energy, deal with stress effectively and create a healthy work life balance are... (e.g. I can do, wear, have …)
e.g. To not have to constantly worry about food, weight and eating	*e.g.To be able to wake up in the morning feeling great and energised for the day ahead*

When you do this exercise, you'll find that one of the sources of motivation; towards or away-from is easier for you to work with than the other. Make sure that you complete the exercise. The more effort put into this part of the process, the stronger your foundation for effective and permanent lifestyle change.

To crank up the pain, I just want to make a delicate point about the importance of a healthy body image. By turning up to important business meetings with a body image that loudly trumpets "neglect", what sort of message are you really sending to prospects and clients? I call this "the elephant in the meeting room". Enough said...

Now stop reading for a couple of minutes and come up with at least 2 SMART goals for your Fit For Business programme. To make them SMART, the goals should be:
Specific
Measurable
Achievable
Realistic
Time-bound

e.g. *To lose 30lbs before our summer holiday in July and keep it off*

Do make sure that your goals are clear and specific. A goal is sometimes defined as a dream with a deadline. Being lean and healthy is a dream. Losing 40 lbs by my 40th birthday is a goal.

Now, please ask yourself what has stopped you being energetic, fully managing stress and enjoying a healthy work life balance in the past.

What do you fear might happen in the process of changing your lifestyle? Really give this some thought and again, please stop and write down your thoughts.

This last question should help you understand any "limiting beliefs" about your ability to deal with stress and create a healthy work life balance.

Week 2 – Drink The Right Amount Of Water, Daily

This is the easiest and yet the most important way to gain energy, deal with stress and feel great, as long as you take it sensibly and gradually.

Approximately 60% of the body and 70% of the brain is made up of water, so think of your system as a river. If you're feeling overweight and lacking natural vitality, your own river is very likely to be slow-moving, somewhat stagnant and full of toxins. To feel more energetic and less stressed, it's really important to get the river flowing, so as to begin to move toxins out of the body. In medical speak, the kidneys need sufficient water to rid the body of toxic waste. Urine should be almost clear or very pale yellow.

According to Dr F Batmanghelidj, water shortage is the background to most of the health problems in our society. Dr Batman, as he is affectionately known, trained as a conventional Doctor at a London Medical School. He has challenged the medical and pharmaceutical establishment with some amazing and practical information about the importance of proper hydration. You can read firsthand what he has to say at www.watercure.com. In the book "Water Cures and Drugs Kill, Dr Batman explains why dehydration is a main cause of pain and disease.

You can go to www.watercure.com/wondersofwater.html and download a free 3-part audio interview by Tony Robbins with Dr Batman (it's on the left of the page). The sound quality is not perfect, but the information is life changing, so please do listen to that interview and most importantly, *act on the information.*

If you'd like more compelling facts about the amazing health properties of water, visit the website of The International Water For Life Foundation.

How much water should I be drinking a day?
Half your body weight in lbs indicates the bare minimum amount of water you should be drinking a day in ounces. In order to enjoy optimal health, most people should drink 2-3 litres of water each day. Work up gradually and your body will develop a natural craving for water. Drink some water every two hours, but not during a meal, as this may inhibit efficient digestion.

It's best to use a simple daily chart to log your intake of water during the first four days when re-hydrating the body. When you drink water, make a note of the time and how much water you consume in centilitres.

Day & Date	Time	Centilitres of Water Taken
Daily Total (aim for 2-3 litres)		

Day & Date	Time	Centilitres of Water Taken
Daily Total (aim for 2-3 litres)		

Day & Date	Time	Centilitres of Water Taken
Daily Total (aim for 2-3 litres)		

Day & Date	Time	Centilitres of Water Taken
Daily Total (aim for 2-3 litres)		

Why should I fill in a water chart?

Dr Batman says that people don't tend to know that they are dehydrated and this is especially a challenge for busy business people. If you are waiting for a dry mouth, it's already too late; we don't manifest dehydration by a dry mouth. So, the body isn't able to regulate its water intake. You will initially have to "force" yourself to drink 2-3 litres of water a day, before the body begins to crave water naturally after a few days. Experiments with elderly people have found that they can easily become severely dehydrated without realising.

It's important not to drink too much water however as your body needs the correct proportion of essential salts in order to be healthy – no more than 4 litres each day (you'll find that very hard to do without becoming a bathroom recluse anyway)

If the body doesn't have an adequate supply of pure water (not soft drinks fruit juices, tea, coffee and alcohol), it can't break down and use food. It's water alone, not other drinks that meets the body's requirements. An exception is pure vegetable juices, which may comprise some of your water intake. If you feel like a hot drink, try Rooibos (Red Bush) Tea, which is as hydrating as water.

The health benefits of Red Bush Tea are quite impressive :-
Contains similar amounts of **polyphenols** and has been shown to be anti-carcinogenic, anti-mutagenic, anti-inflammatory and anti-viral activity.

Naturally caffeine-free so is ideal for people who want to cut back on caffeine or want to drink it before going to bed. Actually it's recommended you drink Rooibos before going to bed as it can help with insomnia. It's also very low in tannins.

Contains calcium and manganese to help build strong teeth and bones.

Can be given to babies suffering from colic, sleeping problems or stomach cramps. Simply add some milk to the tea.

Contains alpha hydroxyl acid and zinc which is great for the skin. You can even apply it directly to the skin to help with acne, eczema and sunburn etc.

People with kidney stones can drink it because there's no oxalic acid.

Full of vitamins and minerals such as zinc, copper, calcium, manganese, magnesium, potassium.

Gently alkalizing to the body (see week 3 for an explanation)

The body manifests dehydration in different ways:-
Tiredness in the evening after work or in the morning.
The feeling that you don't have the energy to get out of bed.
Feeling flushed, dejected, depressed, anxious and irritable.
At more severe levels of dehydration, the lungs begin to shut down and severe medical conditions can arise. Angina, shortness of breath, heart failure, MS, Parkinson's Disease, Alzheimer's Disease and even cancer can be complications of dehydration.

Water is the main energiser in the body. It produces hydro-electric energy at the cellular level, in the brain and in the nervous system. Your 50 trillion brain and nerve cells need a great deal of energy and rely on the hydro-electric energy produced by water. By hydrating properly, blood becomes less viscous and cholesterol levels will be healthy. No need for blood thinners and cholesterol-reducing drugs.

Proper hydration on a regular basis provides the foundation for your Fit For Business Program.
To survive, you can lose:-
50% of your glucose
50% of your fat
50% of your protein
But only 20% of your water

To gain energy and help deal with stress, drink 2-3 litres of pure water, evenly-paced throughout the day. Drink water when you awake in the morning, as the body will have begun to dehydrate during sleep.

As mentioned already, it's important not to drink more than 4 litres of water a day, as this can leave your body short of essential salts and set up health challenges elsewhere.

Depending on where you live, it may be perfectly safe to drink filtered tap water at home, or if you prefer, drink bottled water which is slightly alkaline. See p65-68 of The pH Miracle for Weight Loss by Dr R Young and Shelley Young for a full list of bottled waters and their alkalinity. Vitel and Evian for example are listed as mildly alkaline. For proper hydration to be even more effective in terms of energy gain and weight loss, it really does help to drink water which is slightly alkaline

One way to produce alkaline water is with a water ionizer. Popular in the United States, most models are over $2000 to install in the home. For around one-quarter of the cost of a water ionizer, another good option is to install a water revitalizer, which adds 25% more oxygen and also naturally softens the water at the same time. A few years ago, I fitted one of these into the supply pipe at the stopcock inside the house (a very simple process which can be reversed if you move) and the results have been excellent. To find out more, visit:
http://www.AndrewBridgewater.com/water

Add powdered wheatgrass to your water for extra energy. Start slowly by dissolving a teaspoon of wheatgrass in a litre of water, twice daily. Then gradually increase the strength to 2 teaspoons of wheatgrass in a litre of water, twice daily. In the next section, I'll explain why and how this works.

Week 3 – Alkalise To Add Vitality

I'm about to reveal a powerful secret to lifelong health and wellness that few people know about. If you understand and <u>act on it</u>, this information will change your life. It will help you enjoy an optimal weight and more energy than ever before.

According to the renowned chemist and microbiologist, Dr Robert O Young, author of "The pHMiracle" and "Sick and Tired", the body strives to maintain a delicate acid/alkaline balance. In order to be vibrant, lean and healthy, your body needs to maintain a blood pH level in the range 7.360-7.370. (*pH* is the measure of the acidity or alkalinity of a solution and stands for the power of Hydrogen)

The pH scale goes from 0 (highly acidic) to 14 (highly alkaline).

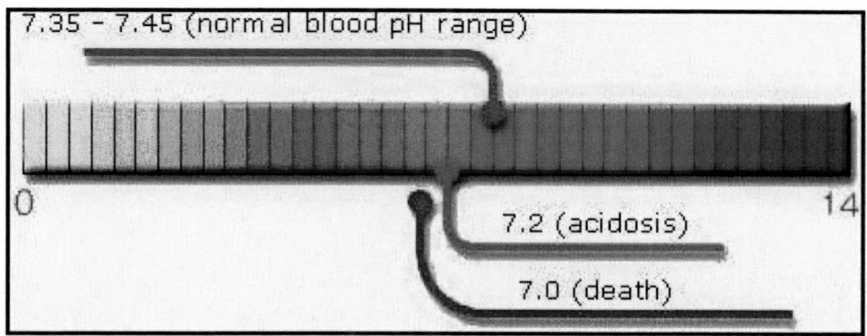

Your bloodstream needs to maintain a slightly alkaline pH balance of 7.365 in order to work best and for you to be lean and healthy. Lower and to the left is too acidic and higher and to the right is too alkaline (neither of which is a good thing).

If your pH level is too acidic, then the body is lethargic and creates fat. This is to isolate dangerous acidity away from the vital organs, in the form of fat around the middle (remember acid burns).

So, low energy levels, high stress and excess weight are often symptoms of a deeper underlying problem. You <u>must</u> deal with the underlying problem (an over-acidic diet and lifestyle).

Put simply, high stress, drinking acidic beverages and eating acidic foods adds to the acidity of your blood. De-stressing, drinking alkaline water and eating alkalising foods adds to the alkalinity of your blood. I'm going to list some common acid and alkaline foods and drinks.

Examples of Common Food & Drink Types that have a Strongly Acid pH	Examples of Common Food & Drink Types that are Mildly Acidic	Examples of Common Food & Drink Types that are Mildly Alkaline	Examples of Common Food & Drink Types that are Strongly Alkaline
red meat	grains	tofu	soy
alcohol	legumes	vegetables	vegetables
eggs	most nuts	olive oil	real salt
dried fruit	canola oil	goat milk	sprouts
sugars	fruit juice	almonds	garlic
hard cheese	milk, rice/ soy milk	buckwheat	alkaline water

So, if you'd rather feel energetic ,less stressed and lose that "business belly", it's much better to tackle the root causes, rather than the symptoms (another reason most diets don't work is that they target symptoms and the effects can be short-lived). To gain energy and lose weight for good, your blood pH level needs to move further up the scale into the optimal range of 7.360-7.370 and remain there.

Therefore, if you want to deal with stress at the source, simply change what you eat and drink, so as to reduce acidity and increase alkalinity. Another benefit is that the body has no reason to hold onto any fat which is there to protect vital organs and body tissues from the harmful effects of acidity (as I said, acid burns). The beauty of this approach is that it's entirely natural and healthy; your body just needs to find its own balance. When it does, fat will literally "melt" away over a few months, faster if you metabolise it away through sensible amounts of exercise (I will talk more about this later in the program).

You can either store poisonous acids in your fat or "pee your way to good health" – it's your choice! While we're on the subject (and I won't dwell on it), you will visit the bathroom more when starting to drink 2-3 litres of water a day. However, the kidneys and bladder will strengthen and the body adapts quickly to needing and valuing proper hydration.

Remember, its water you need for your 2-3 litres a day. Amazingly, it takes 32 glasses of alkaline water to neutralise just one glass of pH 2.5 cola.

So how do I become more alkaline and less acidic?

Incorporate more alkalising foods and drinks (aim for 75% by volume) in your diet and less acidic foods and drinks (aim for 25% by volume). I'll share some more specific ideas now.

ALKALIZING VEGETABLES	ALKALIZING FRUITS	ALKALIZING PROTEIN
Alfalfa	Apple	Almonds
Barley Grass	Apricot	Chestnuts
Beets	Avocado	Millet
Beet Greens	Banana (no brown spots)	Tofu (fermented)
Broccoli	Berries	Soya
Cabbage	Blackberries	**ALKALIZING SPICES AND SEASONINGS**
Carrot	Cantaloupe	Cinnamon
Cauliflower	Cherries, sour	Curry
Celery	Coconut, fresh	Ginger
Chard Greens	Currants	Mustard
Chlorella	Dates, dried	Chili Pepper
Collard Greens	Figs, dried	Sea Salt
Cucumber	Grapes	Miso
Dandelions	Grapefruit	Tamari
Eggplant	Honeydew Melon	All Herbs
Garlic	Lemon	**ALKALIZING OTHER**
Green Beans	Lime	Cider Vinegar
Green Peas	Muskmelons	Bee Pollen
Kale	Nectarine	Probiotic Cultures
Kohlrabi	Orange	Soya Milk
Lettuce	Peach	Green Juices
Mushrooms	Pear	Veggie Juices
Onions	Pineapple	Fresh Fruit Juice
Parsnips	Raisins	Mineral Water
Peas	Raspberries	Alkaline Antioxidant Water
Peppers	Rhubarb	**ALKALIZING SWEETENERS**
Pumpkin	Strawberries	Stevia, honey, palm sugar,
Radishes	Tangerine	
Rutabaga	Tomato	
Spinach	Tropical Fruits	
Sprouts	Plums	
Sweet potatoes	Watermelon	
Tomatoes		
Watercress		
Wheat Grass		

ACIDIFYING VEGETABLES	**ACIDIFYING NUTS and BUTTERS**	**ACIDIFYING BEANS & LEGUMES**
Corn	Cashews	Black Beans
Olives	Peanuts	Chick Peas
Winter Squash	Peanut Butter	Green Peas
ACIDIFYING	Pecans	Kidney Beans
FRUITS	Walnuts	Lentils
Blueberries	**ACIDIFYING**	Red Beans
Canned or Glazed	**ANIMAL PROTEIN**	Soy Beans
Fruits	Bacon	White Beans
Cranberries	Beef	Rice Milk
Currants	Cod	Almond Milk
Plums	Corned Beef	**ACIDIFYING DAIRY**
Prunes	Haddock	Butter
ACIDIFYING	Lamb	Cheese
GRAINS, GRAIN	Lobster	Ice Cream
PRODUCTS	Mussels	Ice Milk
Amaranth	Offal	**ACIDIFYING FATS**
Barley	Oyster	**& OILS**
Bran, wheat	Pork	Butter
Bran, oat	Rabbit	Canola Oil
Corn	Salmon	Corn Oil
Hemp Seed Flour	Sardines	Hemp Seed Oil
Oats (rolled)	Sausage	Flax Oil
Oatmeal	Scallops	Lard
Quinoa	Shrimp	Olive Oil
Rice (all)	Scallops	Safflower Oil
Rice Cakes	Shellfish	Sesame Oil
Rye	Tuna	Sunflower Oil
Wheat	Turkey	**ACIDIFYING**
Wheat Germ	Veal	**SWEETENERS**
Noodles	Venison	Carob
Macaroni	**ACIDIFYING**	Sugar
Spaghetti	**ALCOHOL**	Corn Syrup
Bread	Beer	**ACIDIFYING**

Crackers	Spirits	**OTHER FOODS**
Flour, white	Wine	Cocoa
Flour, wheat		Coffee
		Vinegar
		Mustard
		Soft Drinks

Ensure that you are alkalising and energising your body by reducing the intake of acidic foods and drinks and increasing the intake of alkalising foods and drinks.

So to repeat: for most people, the ideal diet is 75% alkalising by volume and 25% acidifying by volume.

Week 4 – Eat A Proper Balanced Diet

Before you reach the "Tipping Point" and are making your own healthy choices routinely and easily (that won't be long), it helps to bear in mind that "nothing tastes as good as looking good feels". A proper balanced diet makes sure that you live with more energy and detoxifies the blood.

Here are some top dietary tips for optimal pH nutrition, promoting energy gain and rapid weight loss:-
Eat more green vegetables with high water content to help alkalise and energise your body every day. 70% of your diet should be water-rich foods, allowing your body to be cleansed, not clogged.

Drink 2-3 litres of pure or better still, alkalised water with wheatgrass at regular intervals, each day.

Significantly cut down on processed foods. All of these contain additives and toxins, making it harder to lose your business belly, whatever the fat content of the processed food. Remember that you are what you eat and drink and to enjoy high performance from your body, it's important to fuel it properly.

Eat good fats and oils (mono and polyunsaturated). The brain is 70% fat and 30% water. The right sort of fats and oils are essential for the manufacture of hormones, as a carrier of vitamins and they help keep body tissues and cells in good repair. Approximately 20% of your calories should come from healthy fats which will help you to feel fuller, as well as look and feel younger. They lubricate joints and provide energy, help to relieve arthritis, asthma, PMS, allergies, skin conditions and improve brain functioning. They protect your heart and circulatory system, protect against illness and depression, support the immune system and help your skin, nails and hair to look great – quite an impressive list of benefits.

Fats and oils are either saturated or unsaturated. Saturated fats tend to be solid at room temperature and animal fats are mostly saturated. It's unsaturated fats that are the healthy ones; these are categorised as either monounsaturated or polyunsaturated. Monounsaturated fats and oils include omega 3 and omega 6, which your body can't produce without ingesting them. Eat avocados and oily fish, such as mackerel and salmon – aim for 3-5 servings a week and it may help to take an omega 3 and 6 supplement daily. A simple healthy-eating tip is to drizzle cold-pressed extra virgin olive oil over vegetables and salads. Polyunsaturated oils include sesame seed oil and sunflower oil.

Eat plenty of fibre. This is essential to keep food moving through the digestive tract. Also, fibre-rich foods fill you up and, like water, help you feel full. Aim to consume about 25g of fibre each day. Most business leaders could lose approximately 10lb of weight in a year, just by doubling their fibre intake. Fibre is only found in plant foods – fruits, vegetables, grains and cereals - we're unable to digest it, so it's just eliminated. Great tasting sources of fibre include high-fibre cereals, oatmeal (4g of fibre per cup) apples (3g of fibre each), broccoli, black beans (15g of fibre per cup), nuts, chickpeas and lentils. It's best to take fibre in the morning for breakfast and in the evening too.

There are two main types of fibre: water soluble and insoluble. You can get soluble fibre from all sorts of fruit, oats, barley and root crops. Soluble fibre encourages the growth of healthy bacteria that help digestion. Insoluble fibre is the "crunchy" kind which you can get from wheat, bran, nuts, seeds and some vegetables, such as celery and green beans. Insoluble fibre passes from one end of the digestive tract to the other virtually unchanged, performing a "clean sweep" of your digestive tract.

Apart from improving the digestive process and helping you feel fuller for longer, fibre has 3 other important roles:

1. It improves protein absorption by slowing down the rate at which proteins move through the digestive tract. This way, the body is able to maximise protein absorption.
2. Soluble fibre helps carbohydrates to be used for energy production, rather than be stored as body fat.
3. Fibre builds immunity by helping the body rid itself of harmful bacteria, viruses and allergens. Taking in more fibre increases your chances of staying healthy at all times and you will be eating the kinds of foods that add vitality and energise you. Altogether, a brilliant way to look and feel great!

As with the other steps in The Fit For Business Program, take it steady and increase your consumption of fibre gradually, adding 2-3 g per day each week. So, if your current intake is 10g per day, go for 12 g in week 1, 14g in week 2 and so on, until your daily intake is around 25g or more. Fibre works more effectively with liquids and by this point, you will already by hydrating properly.

Eat only lean protein. Like fibre and water, lean protein keeps you feeling fuller for longer and helps to maintain muscle mass, which in turn helps to burn fat. Excellent sources of protein include soya and soya-based products (vegetable soya is over 40% protein; higher than meat or fish), skinless chicken and turkey, fish, lentils, kidney beans and tofu. Look for fermented soya if you can and ensure it's organic in origin.

Always eat a good breakfast and eat at regular intervals during the day. 4-5 small meals each day are better than 2-3 large ones when it comes to energy gain and weight loss. After fasting for 10 hours or so, it's important to set yourself up for the day with a good breakfast. Avoid the "Full English" and eat a high-fibre cereal such as All-Bran, Bran Flakes, Shredded Wheat or something similar, followed by brown toast. Try poached eggs on brown toast if you fancy something cooked. As an alternative, try fruit for breakfast on its own. I'll say more about this when we come to look at correct food combining next week.

Take a few supplements every day. Take a multivitamin which includes iron and also a zinc supplement to build the immune system. Multivitamins and mineral supplements will help boost your energy levels and help stop you falling prey to those minor ailments. It's also a good idea to take a fish oil supplement with omega 3 and 6; great for stabilising mood, adding vitality and all round wellbeing. Finally, aloe-vera has great detoxifying and laxative properties; it helps to improve the efficiency of the colon which, as we'll see, is important for great health.

Week 5 – The Power Of Proper Food Combining

The chances are you haven't previously heard about this fantastic way to deal with stress and feel more energetic quickly.

Proper combining of foods creates optimal digestion. Have you ever wondered why sometimes you feel very tired after eating a meal, especially one containing a range of food types?

Dr William Hay introduced the idea of proper food combining in 1911. His ideas fit with those of Dr Robert Young, in that he believed there is one underlying cause of health problems – over-acidification of the body and blood. Proper food combining helps ensure that the body maintains its natural and delicate chemical balance.

Dr Hay classified foods into three types according to their chemical requirements for efficient digestion:

1. Alkaline-forming foods such as fruits and vegetables. Even acid tasting fruits such as lemons result in the production of alkaline salts in the body
2. Concentrated proteins such as meat, fish, eggs and cheese which are acid-forming in the digestive process
3. Concentrated carbohydrates or starch foods are acid forming. These include grains, bread and all foods containing flour, all sugars and foods containing sugars, other than the naturally occurring sugars found in fruit

Dr Hay's theory is that, although proteins and carbohydrates are acid-forming in digestion, they require different conditions (enzymes) for digestion and should never be combined in the same meal. The main idea is that the human digestive system is not designed for complex meals; we are capable of digesting many different kinds of foods, but not all at once. The reason that you can sometimes feel tired after a meal is that proteins and carbohydrates require different enzymes to break them down.

Amylase, the enzyme used in the digestion of carbohydrates requires an alkaline environment. Protease which breaks down protein needs an acid environment. Therefore, eating carbohydrates and proteins in the same meal creates something of an "internal war" in your stomach. Both interfere with the digestion of each other, resulting in incomplete digestion of both. Proper food combining involves eating foods that are digested in the same way as part of the same meal. This means maximum nutritional benefits, lower stress for the body and greater vitality.

To make things easy, here's a summary of Dr Hay's rules for healthy food combining:-
Starches and sugars should not be eaten with proteins and acid fruits at the same meal.

Vegetables, salads and fruits (whether acid or sweet) if correctly combined should form the major part of the diet.

Proteins, starches and fats should be eaten in small quantities

Only whole grains and unprocessed starches should be used and refined and processed foods should be significantly reduced, or better still, eliminated from the diet.

Not less than four hours between starch and protein meals.

Milk does not combine well with food and should be kept to a minimum.

Don't mix foods that “fight” in the stomach

List A	List B	List C
Proteins	Neutral Foods	Starches
All meat	Most vegetables	Biscuits
All poultry	All salads	Bread
Cheese	Seeds	Cakes
Eggs	Nuts	Crackers
Fish	Herbs	Oats
Soya Beans	Cream	Pasta
Yoghurt	Butter	Potatoes
	Olive oil	Rice
		Sugar/Honey
		Sweets

Mix any proteins with any neutral foods.

Mix any starches with any neutral foods.

Never mix proteins and starches.

Mix vegetables or salads with pulses i.e. beans/lentils - make these and unprocessed foods the main part of your diet

Food combining is a very effective way of helping to create an alkaline environment in which your body cells can thrive. Proper combining reduces putrefaction in the body, creating a more alkaline condition and resulting in higher energy levels.

Here are just a few great fresh vegetables you can eat freely with proteins or carbohydrates:-

Asparagus
Aubergine
Broccoli
Brussels sprouts
Cabbage
Carrots
Cauliflower
Celery
Cucumber
Green beans
Onions
Parsley
Parsnips
Peas
Peppers – red, yellow and green
Spinach
Swede
Turnip
Water chestnuts

It's generally *not* a good idea to wash food down with a drink, especially cold drinks as the cold shuts down digestive activity. Water and other liquids dilute digestive juices and should be drunk at least half an hour before, or one hour after any meal that includes animal protein. The exception is a few sips of warm water soon after a meal, which can aid digestion.

You don't *have* to food-combine religiously in order to gain energy and lose weight, but it will accelerate progress and is worth experiencing for the results in your body. Try it before an important business meeting or presentation and see how energetic and clear thinking you feel. It's important not to eat late at night, say after 9pm, so that your body has a chance to digest the evening meal before bedtime.

Keeping a food and health journal is a great way of understanding the precise connection between your diet and your health and levels of stress. Write down everything that you eat and drink and make sure that this includes quantities and cooking methods. For example, mention sugar in drinks and oil used in cooking.

Each day, note where, when and why you ate the food or had the drink and how you felt before and after. It's particularly important to note any ill feelings, when they occurred and how long they lasted. Each week, review your journal to see if you can make any connections. For example, did you feel lethargic and tired the next morning after drinking 3 glasses of wine with dinner, did you feel energetic and vibrant after that vegetable juice drink with breakfast and great all day after going to the gym before breakfast?

If you identify a problem food or drink, eliminate it from your diet for a week and monitor the effects. I'm going to share a sample food and health journal. It's worth mentioning that I compiled it whilst on holiday in Cyprus with my sons and there are a few "treats" in there.

Day & Date	Food & Drink Consumed	Energy/Vitality Rating (1-3) & Observations	Learning
Sun 26/10 7am 8.15am	1 glass of water on waking up 1 litre of Wheatgrass in water before 20 minute pre-breakfast walk Breakfast:- All-Bran with Bran Flakes and 2 fresh figs Skimmed milk 2 slices of wholemeal brown toast & Vitalite Margarine with 50% fruit cherry jam 1 cup of weak green tea (no milk)	Felt great at the start of the day and energetic enough to want a walk before breakfast 3 Didn't feel hungry or need anything to eat before lunch at 1pm	Hydrating like this first thing in the morning helps set me up for the day I always feel satisfied by a breakfast which includes plenty of fibre
1pm	Lunch:- Pasta stuffed with spinach and ricotta Toasted Pitta bread and taramasalata Salad (tomatoes, cucumber, lettuce, sliced peppers) 2 pieces of Kinder Bueno chocolate wafer 1 mug of weak Tetley tea with milk	2 Probably ate more pasta than I needed and felt a little lethargic for an hour	Watch portion sizes and stop eating before I feel full
6.30pm	Pre-dinner drink; 1 pint lager Evening meal:- Barbecued chicken kebabs with salad 1 Milky Way 1 cup of green tea	2 Felt quite full after the meal, but energetic enough to get back to writing this afterwards!	On holiday in Cyprus, it's easy to have a beer before dinner. I wouldn't normally do so at home

Energy/Vitality rating, 1=low, 2=medium, 3= high

It's been proven that keeping a food and health journal is much more effective as a means of facilitating healthy and sustainable weight loss than constant use of scales. Research in The American Journal of Preventative Medicine found that those keeping a food diary – (what they ate and rating energy level for the day) can lose up to twice as much weight over a 6-month period than those who don't.

A final point about measuring progress. There will be times when your energy levels and weight seem to level-out or hit a plateau. This is perfectly normal; take comfort from the fact that you have created the perfect foundation to get healthy permanently. This is a good time to measure your waist, thighs, upper arms and neck, as well as to check how your clothes are fitting.

Muscle weighs heavier than fat and if you are taking some sensible exercise and toning the body, this may result in a stabilisation of weight at certain intervals. This can be a great time to get a coach. You can join others in the Fit For Business group coaching program or work one-to-one with me. These are great ways to get accountable, get new motivation and hit your goals faster.

For more information, please visit
http://www.AndrewBridgewater.com/mentoring

Week 6 – Detoxify Daily

Aging is defined by Sang Whang, author of "Reverse Aging" as the accumulation of acid wastes within our body. For more information, please visit his fascinating website at www.sangwhang.org. The theory is that we get old because we are not disposing of all internally generated acid wastes and toxins; these simply accumulate in the body.

We are born with high alkaline blood pH of 7.44 and as we get older, the blood pH drops down to 7.35 or below. This is one of the reasons why younger people are more energetic than older people.

The most effective way of getting rid of all the acid wastes and toxins that have accumulated in the body after years of consuming acidic and toxic foods and drinks is to ***gradually*** reduce their intake. By slowly cleansing the system of toxins, you can actually feel younger and more alive.

Rapid detoxing can lead to unpleasant withdrawal symptoms. If currently drinking 5 cups of coffee or tea each day, try changing to decaffeinated and then reducing consumption to 2 cups a day in the first week and 1 cup a day in the second week. By then, if you have been hydrating properly and acting on the other steps in the Fit For Business program, taste buds may have adapted and the desire to drink coffee or tea will actually diminish.

This is the amazing thing about the formula we are working with; your body and brain will actually adapt and start seeking healthy alternatives to the unhealthy choices you were making before. Yes, you will start to crave healthy alkalising foods and drinks, while beginning to dislike the taste of those old toxic, unhealthy acidic foods and drinks.

Paul, one of my clients found that after following the Fit For Business Program for 3 weeks, he began to dream again for the first time in years! The dreams were pleasant and he even found himself wanting to return to them. It turned out that Paul had gradually reduced his coffee intake from 10 cups a day, to five, to decaffeinated coffee and now he doesn't drink coffee at all.

Many people are simply too toxic to do a 10-day or 20-day detox without suffering significant withdrawal symptoms. The body comes to rely on toxins and will resist letting go of them.

By slowing and ultimately stopping the consumption of toxic foods and drinks, your body no longer has to focus its energy on moving toxins out of the system. The metabolism will then start to burn fat at a much more rapid rate.

For an easy, healthy way to detoxify the colon, try Holland & Barrett's aloe-vera colon cleanse tablets. This is a great way to gradually detoxify the digestive system. Take one a day for a month and then repeat the process every six months. They're good value too; 60 tablets at just under £5 will last a full year, if used as suggested.

So here are three simple detoxing tips to put into action this week:-

1. Slowly reduce and better still completely eliminate caffeine in tea, coffee and any other drinks. Substitute Red Bush, fruit teas or herbal teas instead
2. Reduce consumption of processed foods, all of which contain toxic preservatives and additives (it's those E numbers)
3. If you drink "diet" fizzy drinks – please don't. You're actually better off drinking the full sugar versions if you must - because artificial sweeteners are even more toxic

than sugar. I'll talk more about artificial sweeteners, their risks and the healthier alternatives later in the program.

Week 7 – Having Fun With Exercise

Moderate exercise is alkalising to the body, whereas excessive exercise can actually *create* acidity, due to lactic acid build up and the effects of cortisol.

The trick here is appropriate motivation and it helps to find a form of exercise that works for you as a busy business person. If you've not really tried cycling, I highly recommend it. Invigorating and great for fat burning, cycling outdoors puts you in touch with nature and doesn't put pressure on joints or muscles, unlike running. Or you can always do it indoors on a fixed wheel trainer while watching TV or even while reading this book.

Don't start exercising too vigorously too soon. It's important to follow the advice of your doctor or qualified medical practitioner here.

Business leaders who maintain a healthy lifestyle and maintain an optimal weight regard controlling weight and gaining energy as only two of the benefits of regular exercise. Other reasons to exercise include defeating stress and depression permanently, feeling better overall, sleeping better, getting more done, shaping your legs, living longer and happier, reducing blood pressure and the risk of cardio-vascular problems, getting off prescription drugs, building confidence and gaining mental clarity. That's just for a start!

Even those who don't like to exercise can ultimately fall in love with the benefits; find your own compelling reasons and you can too. Perhaps the most compelling reason for me is to feel and look younger. I highly recommend the book by Dr Henry Lodge and Chris Crowley titled "Younger Next Year: Turn Back Your Biological Clock".

What are your 10 compelling reasons to exercise? Stop for a few minutes and write down your own unique and powerful reasons for getting some sensible exercise. Against each reason, identify whether it's motivated by moving you towards pleasure or away from pain.

Reason to exercise	**Towards Pleasure or Away-from Pain?**
1	
2	
3	
4	
5	
6	
7	
8	
9	
10	

Looking at your own list, which reason really "juices you up"? Which is the one that you'll keep in your head and use whenever you need it? Find a strong enough "why" and you can achieve amazing results. Please don't skimp on this exercise or be tempted to skip it; the technique really works.

If your strongest reason is motivated by moving away from

pain, this could be good to get you started, but moving towards pleasure is what will ultimately keep you exercising. Therefore, look for your strongest reason which is "towards" motivated and taking you towards pleasure. Visualise this one clearly and regularly. Focusing on what we want is far more effective in producing results than focusing on what we don't want.
Here again are some of the well-recognised benefits of sensible aerobic exercise if you still need convincing:
Helps you to eat better, digest better and eliminate waste better.
Helps you to feel better mentally and emotionally
Helps you to sleep better
Helps you to enjoy a more fulfilling love life
Increases your physical attractiveness
Is fantastic for the heart and cardiovascular system:-
Increases your blood supply
Produces healthier body tissues and cells which are supplied with more oxygen
Your lungs will be more efficient
Blood vessels become enlarged and more pliable, reducing the resistance to blood flow

It's important to exercise at the right intensity in order to lose your business belly in the most efficient way possible. Have a look at www.brianmac.co.uk/hrm1.htm to find out more about heart rate training zones and check out the free spreadsheet to calculate your own optimal heart rate for effective energy gain, weight loss and long-term stress management.

To put this information into practice, you'll need to use a heart-rate monitor while exercising. It's a simple device worn like a watch and has a chest strap to pick up the heart rate. A typical heart rate monitor costs around £35. The beauty of this little device is that exercising becomes fun and it is relatively easier to exercise at the optimal level for fat loss. Exercise for 30 minutes or so at least 3 times a week, so that you sweat gently; the monitored heart rate should remain inside your 80% target heart rate zone. This will mean that you burn up to 9 times more calories (a calorie is simply a unit of energy). Dropping your heart rate will not burn nearly as many fat calories and going above your target heart rate can cause the release of cortisol, leading to fat retention around the middle. In other words, if you over-do the exercise, a business belly can become harder to lose. Over-exercise can also lead to lactic acid build up and muscle breakdown.

"Keep fit to avoid cancer" read the front page headline in a UK national newspaper in September 2008. It went on to say that regular exercise will keep cancer at bay according to a ground breaking new study. Moderate amounts of walking, cycling, playing sport, going to the gym or housework can stave off the disease. In the study which followed nearly 80,000 people over a decade, scientists discovered that people who were physically active were protected against a number of common cancers including colon, liver, pancreatic and stomach cancers. The more they exercised, the better they were at staving off cancer. The most active men were 13% less likely to get cancer than the least active men. For women, exercise was **even better** at beating off the disease; the most active women had a 16% lower cancer risk than the least active women.

Research has consistently shown that exercising appropriately and consistently over a 6 month period forms a positive addiction for a lifetime. So, let your own personal compelling reasons get you started and become addicted to the positive benefits of regular exercise.

A 10-year study by Christopher Guerriero, who has developed a programme called "Maximise Your Metabolism", proved that persistence is the single most important part of any diet or exercise programme. The study followed a group (we'll call them Group 1) who exercised and dieted very strictly, but sporadically. Their results were compared to another group

(Group 2) who exercised mildly and followed a very basic diet. However this group never varied their routine. Even though Group 2 exercised and dieted far less than Group 1 (but did so persistently), Group 2 got 68% better results on average that those who exercised and dieted very strictly but sporadically. The message is clear; 30 minutes of gentle sweating 3-4 times a week is far better than a frantic workout every 10 days. Yet more evidence of the power of the slight edge.

Sensible exercise accelerates your ability to lose weight, significantly reduces stress levels and elevates the mood. It's also very important for long-term weight management and for vitality and energy. When you are "mentally" tired at the end of a tough day, physical exercise can often alleviate that tiredness. For a seemingly endless stream of energy and vitality throughout the day, try exercising first thing in the morning. Experience the results in your body and I promise, the effort will be worth it. Your business will thank you for it too.

One final piece of advice on exercise; successful people focus on the outcome they're looking for, not the process of getting there. I wish someone had told me this years ago! The process of getting up half an hour earlier to exercise on a cold, damp morning before breakfast is pretty unappealing for most people, but focus on how great you'll soon be looking and feeling when you do. This way the experience is very different (not to mention the results).

Week 8 - Stress For Success

It's not just what you eat and drink that can create acidity; negative feelings and emotions also have an important part to play. Have you ever been so angry or upset with someone that you literally got an upset stomach? All negative emotions create an acidic environment.

Negative emotions and stress can physiologically change the way our bodies work, making it even more difficult to lose weight, especially around the middle.

How we react to a stressful situation and how we cope with the sources of stress (stressors) in our lives is within our power to influence.

It's useful to think of stress like a bath filling up with water. If water continues to come into the bath faster than it leaves, the bath will overflow and you may experience symptoms of stress and feel stressed.

The link between stress and weight gain is down to the adrenal glands. These glands react when the body is stressed by producing the acid hormones adrenaline and cortisol. Adrenaline causes symptoms of increased heart rate and raised blood pressure.

Cortisol is often referred to as the "stress hormone" and high levels can affect the body's metabolism, by storing fat in order to protect the vital organs. This is why the core area around the middle of the body is often the most difficult place from which to lose weight.

The best way to counteract problems caused by adrenaline and cortisol is to deal with the root causes, rather than the symptoms.

Learn to manage your stress levels well. Following the steps in "Fit For Business" will help you do this naturally at source, before stress becomes a problem. Eating and drinking well, throughout the day as well as exercising sensibly are the most effective ways of ensuring that the body's metabolism is maintained.

Learn a simple meditation process and spend 15 minutes a day doing it. I particularly like Deepak Chopra's 21 Meditation Series because 21 days are all you need to form this powerful and positive habit for a lifetime of mental clarity and happiness. Try it and see.

Recognise how stress affects your body, manage stress effectively and proactively, follow the tips in this program and watch the weight come off and the energy stockpile.

You'll be happier, healthier and more fun to live with too.

Stop for a moment and write your answer to the question "how do you experience stress in your body"?

For some people, stress creates headaches, neck pain, difficulty in sleeping etc. Understanding your own response to stress is an important first step to handling it better.

Again, pause for a few moments and write down your personal stressors (the things causing you to feel stress).

These may be the many different tasks you have to juggle, finding time for yourself and so on.

Finally, what helps you deal with stress?

Good nutrition, proper hydration, sensible regular exercise, daily meditation or relaxation, maintaining friendships and good relationships; all of these are excellent ways of heading off stress before it becomes a problem.

A useful question to ask yourself is:-
"What did I do in the last 24 hours that increased my energy or decreased my energy?" Make a note of the answer to this question for a few days and you will end up with an invaluable list of things you that make you feel tired or energised. Then, just do less of the energy-sapping things and more of the energy-giving things.

For example:-

- When I drink enough water, my energy increases
- When I meditate, I sleep more soundly and feel less irritable
- Eating too much at a time or combining protein and carbohydrate dents my energy levels
- Staying up late can negatively affects tomorrow's energy.
- Exercising in the morning before breakfast makes me feel energised and clearheaded. This actually saves time by increasing productivity during the whole day.

Do this simple exercise and your own observations will be quite revealing.

Simply reduce the negative factors and do more of the positive ones.

My friend Ken Donaldson came up with the following great tips for a stress-free day and I thought you'd appreciate them:

1. Walk into the day...don't run. Meditation and a nice walk are great foundational pieces to start a stress free day, as is nice slow music.

2. Under-expect. Make your "list" no longer than three items...then add another, if you need to. Create success and celebrate your accomplishments.

3. Give yourself extra time. Always give yourself an extra 15 - 30 minutes for a task or a trip.

4. Nothing but the facts. Avoid unnecessary emotional drama from others. Ask them for the facts and work towards a solution. Too many people want to focus only on the problem and all the drama that can surround it.

Detach when you need to.

5. Make lunchtime a time for lunch. Relax for lunch...that's what it's for. Working during lunch is stressful for your digestive system...and puts a strain on your brain.

6. Say "no." Too many people operate from guilt and obligation and don't feel like they can say "no." Practice and become an expert at "no." Likewise, say "yes" to all life-sustaining and energising activities.

7. No Overtime (at home or at work). Start with "no" here. If you're working, leave work when you're supposed to. All work and no play not only makes Jill dull and no fun, it also burns her out. Find some time for your favourite hobby.

8. Relax. Learn to relax on breaks and even when you're driving. Create your relaxing environment with music, aroma, audio books or even silence. Give yourself huge doses of relaxation and some "me time" every day.

9. Presence. Be present with whomever you're with. Turn off the news and anything else that will distract you. Enjoy the company of others 100%. This is some of the best Soul Food you can get.

10. Sleep. Wind down in the evening and set yourself up for good sleep and rest.

Week 9 – Copy Winners, Not Whingers!

Something magical happens when we learn from the success of others. To become truly successful in pretty-much any area of life, it's important to surround yourself with people who are already successful. This is particularly true for health and work life balance. No doubt you've found that almost everyone has an opinion on the subjects. However, take only the advice of others who are lean, fit and healthy themselves and whom you <u>know</u> to be knowledgeable about health and wellness.

Surround yourself with winners and model (copy) those who are already getting great results. If your goal is to weigh 160lb or 11.5 stone by eating healthily and leading an energy-rich life, then seek out other business colleagues and their families who also live a healthy lifestyle. Find out what they eat and drink, spend their time doing and what motivates them. Consistently spending time with people who just talk about getting in shape but never take persistent action, or who just criticise your ideas and efforts, won't make it easier for you to change your busy business lifestyle.

This is a great time to get a Buddy or a Coach to help.

If you want to go further, get a Coach to support you and hold you accountable for results. This way, you'll find it much easier to stick with the small daily changes covered here until they become familiar patterns and habits. So getting a Coach who has already successfully implemented healthy lifestyle choices is a great way of accelerating your progress. For more information about Fit For Business coaching check out http://www.FitForBusiness.tv

As a reader of this book and for a limited time only, you can apply for a free personal coaching session by leaving your details at http://www.AndrewBridgewater.com/Mentoring

I work with a team of highly experienced coaches who have already successfully made the changes you need to implement. If you like what you experience, I or one of my colleagues can work with you in a coaching group or one-to-one whichever you prefer.

Week 10 - SuperFoods That Can Change Your Life

By now it will have become very clear that you are what you think, drink and eat because every cell in the body regenerates over a 2-year period. Whatever situation your body is in now can be changed by implementing the small slight edge changes we've discussed in previous weeks.

I want to share some leading edge information about three foods which truly are SuperFoods in that they are excellent for your long-term health and wellbeing. They are foods that have been proven to help prevent and even reverse chronic health conditions which can occur at any time of life, including heart disease, cancer, hypertension and even dementia. These foods can help to change your body chemistry at the cellular level. But it's not just about avoiding disease – this is about reclaiming your birthright of living with vitality and energy. The three SuperFoods I'm going to talk about may well be a part of your daily nutrition in some form already. In this case, the purpose of discussing them in some depth is to ensure that they remain so for life.

Broccoli
Broccoli is highly alkalising and is packed with fibre, folic acid, iron, calcium and vitamins C & K. It's also one of the most nutrient dense foods offering a very high level of nutrition for a very low calorific cost. I've deliberately avoided mentioning calories until now, but you should know that it actually takes more units of energy (calories) to digest broccoli than are contained in the vegetable – so you could say that it's a negative calorie food!

You might be interested to know that broccoli is the vegetable with the strongest inverse association with colon cancer – even more so if you're under 65 with a history of smoking. So if you've ever smoked, definitely make sure that you eat broccoli.

Eat broccoli both raw and cooked to get the maximum benefits. Raw broccoli is delicious with your favourite low-fat dip or in salads. Broccoli is a great addition to stir-fries. It's also a terrific bone-builder, so your children will really benefit from eating more of what you're eating.

Spinach
Spinach is high in plant-derived omega-3 fatty acids, vitamins B, C & E, calcium, iron and zinc. Popeye was right! – spinach is extremely good for you.

As with broccoli, former smokers in particular can benefit from the power of spinach. Scientific studies have found that those eating a serving of spinach, even if they're former smokers, have a significantly reduced risk of developing lung cancer. It's thought to be the phytonutrients – non vitamin and non mineral compounds found in spinach that are responsible.

Make sure that spinach is washed thoroughly before being cooked or chopped in a salad. Again spinach is best eaten both cooked and raw in salads to ensure that the vitamin C and folic acid content are preserved. Great ways to include spinach in cooking are to layer it in a lasagne, add a handful to soups, add chopped spinach to an omelette. It's also delicious shredded or chopped in a salad.

Oranges
Oranges, tangerines, mandarins and clementines are high in fibre, vitamin C, folic acid, potassium and pectin (a dietary fibre which is very effective in helping to reduce cholesterol). Just one navel orange provides over half of the recommended daily dose of vitamin C for an adult.

Most people are not getting enough vitamin C from dietary sources. Meanwhile, oranges are easy to eat with any meal or as a snack, tasty, juicy and very good for you in many other ways, so make it a habit to eat one every day. If that's not always possible, drink a good quality orange juice which contains the pulp. Despite tasting acidic, oranges are alkalising to the body and help to head off a host of chronic ailments including cancer, strokes and diabetes.

When shopping for oranges, it's worth knowing that the heavier and smaller the fruit (and generally, the thinner the skin), the more juice it contains. Grated orange peel (zest) is a wonderful and healthy ingredient for cakes and fruit salad.

Week 11 – Does Being Fit For Business Lead To More Success?

In a word, **Yes**, though what follows isn't a lesson in Economics. I simply want to top up your motivation to keep on with what you've started. Getting to week 11 is a tremendous achievement in itself and having put the previous 10 weeks of information into daily practice, you will be seeing, feeling and experiencing massive benefits by now.

A recent study in the British Medical Journal found that the healthier you are, the wealthier you become. Researchers examined the link between health and wealth in rich countries, and found that healthier people are more productive, earn more and don't take as much time off work. All fairly obvious really.

It may seem obvious, but an investment in health and managing stress produces big returns for you, your family and your business. Conversely, lose your health and you lose everything – just ask someone who is depressed or chronically ill.

Exercise and healthy eating on a regular basis improve the blood flow within the organ most vital to your business success...the brain. It's quite reasonable to desire more money and more success, but the very first steps should be incorporating a sustainable healthy lifestyle into your schedule – just as you are doing now.

A quick question for you:
Have you ever been at work and eaten an unhealthy lunch or snack while sitting at your desk? (99% of you are answering yes right now - we all do it)

What follows this snack or meal however, is what we are talking about...Did you feel lethargic, unexcited about work and uninspired? Chances are you did.

Conversely, if you ate a healthy lunch and went for a walk, you would have come back rejuvenated, feeling positive and thinking clearly.

Here are a few interesting facts to ponder

1. People that are fit and healthy earn more money
2. People that are fit and healthy run more efficient businesses
3. People that are healthy typically experience less stress
4. People that are fit have a more positive outlook on life

So, if you'd prefer to have more money, a better business, less stress and a better outlook on life, incorporate a healthy Fit For Business routine into your lifestyle permanently. You'll be glad you did!

Week 12 – Keeping It Together

Congratulations – you've arrived at week 12! That means unless you've fast-forwarded to this point, you're one of "the few who do, versus the many who just talk". Taking action and consistently following through are what get results and if you've done just that, you'll have some great results by now.

As you'll have found, it's not necessary to stop eating, drinking or doing everything you had previously done. But you've made some simple changes and are now experiencing the results (isn't it great when others notice and compliment you?)

Your mind and body will ultimately thank you for leading a healthy lifestyle, especially in your 40s and 50s. A recent study from University College London found that a good diet, regular exercise and adopting other lifestyle habits such as stress management techniques can keep biological age down. The research looked at 100,000 people with an average age of 44. Those who led a healthy lifestyle were more likely to remain free of disease and disability over the 17 year duration of the study. Lifestyle was **the** determining factor in how well people aged.

The key principles we've been working with for the last 12 weeks are very well summarised in a diagram I call the cycle of good health.

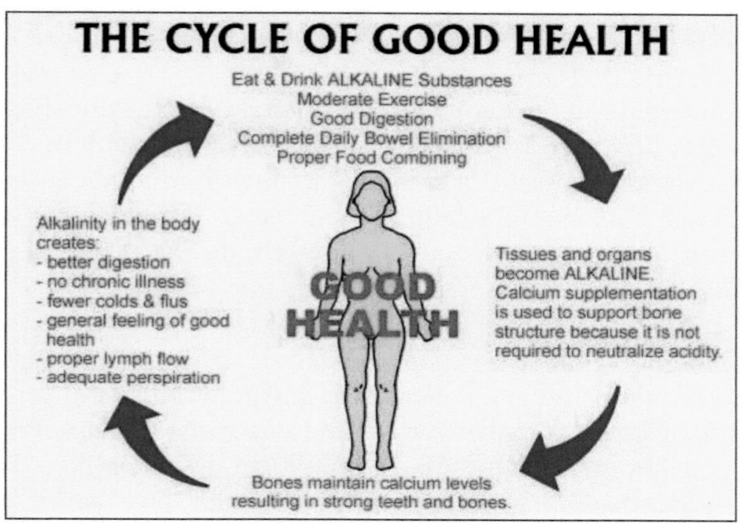

THE CYCLE OF GOOD HEALTH
Eat & Drink ALKALINE Substances
Moderate Exercise
Good Digestion
Complete Daily Bowel Elimination
Proper Food Combining
Alkalinity in the body creates:
- better digestion
- no chronic illness
- fewer colds & flus
- general feeling of good health
- proper lymph flow
- adequate perspiration
GOOD HEALTH
Tissues and organs become ALKALINE.
Calcium supplementation is used to support bone structure because it is not required to neutralize acidity.
Bones maintain calcium levels resulting in strong teeth and bones.

This book and other Fit For Business products and services have been developed to help you introduce a lifestyle that is nurturing and supportive. To find out more about The Fit For Business coaching programme, seminars and retreats, please visit http://www.FitForBusiness.tv

I designed and put together this program to help business leaders just like you massively enhance their lives - permanently.

It'd be a privilege to connect and I'd be delighted to hear about your journey and your success.
Please contact me Andrew@AndrewBridgewater.com

In the remainder of this book, I'll cover information and techniques on how to deal with stress and create a healthy work life balance that will be so much easier to implement now that you have a strong Fit For Business foundation in place.

Chapter 3 – What Exactly Is Stress?

We experience the negative effects of stress when something in the world out there exceeds our self-perceived capacity to cope. Under stress our mind and body produce hormones such as cortisol and adrenaline which in the context of our 50,000 year old physiology are designed to help us fight the threat or flee from it.

Intriguingly, without any stress whatsoever in our lives, we soon become bored and listless. When life becomes too certain and predictable, we crave variety and uncertainty. Yet with too much variety, we crave some certainty and predictability. This is one of the great paradoxes of life and one which it's important to be aware of. Think about it for a moment. If you can't be certain that the ceiling in the room where you're having an important business meeting is going to hold up for the duration, can you relax and focus on the content of the meeting? Of course not.

One of the best ways to understand the key principles of stress is through a metaphor – that of a bath. Water comes into the bath through the taps and the rate at which water flows into the bath is determined by how we experience the many potential stressors or sources of stress in our lives. What forms a stressor for one person won't necessarily do so for another person because we're unique in our perceptions and experiences. Water leaves the bath though the plughole and the rate at which water escapes the plug hole is determined by our ability to deal with the stressors or things that create stress in our lives. Things like holidays, exercise, relaxation and spending time with friends and family outside of work are all examples of ways in which we can diffuse the perception and effects of stress i.e. in terms of the metaphor how water can be helped to flow more effectively through the plughole.

Problems occur when the rate at which water is flowing into the bath exceeds the rate at which it can escape through the plughole (ignoring the overflow pipe for a moment). Water overflows the sides of the bath and we experience the inconvenient and negative effects of stress. These effects are different for everyone. Earlier I encouraged you to make a list of the things that are causing stress in your life right now and the ways in which you are alleviating the effects of stress. Given that we can only change what we're aware of, it's very important to have a good understanding of the stressors and stress-alleviators in your life at any point in time.

Stress Is The Cause Of 99% Of Illness

If the negative effects of stress continue to be experienced over a prolonged period of time (again depending on the individual), the impact is more profound and much more damaging. All of us have what I like to call a "crack of least resistance" or a way in which the negative effects of stress will find a way to manifest in the mind and/or the body. Society seems to be more comfortable dealing with physical manifestations in the body such as heart attacks, strokes, cancer and diabetes. But the crack of least resistance might be in the mental arena where a person has otherwise strong physical health. Both are potentially very dangerous and even life-threatening.

According to http://www.time-to-change.org.uk/ around 1 in 4 people will experience a significant mental health problem at some point in their lives and this is most likely to arise as a result of the negative effects of stress.

So if you want to enjoy good health in business and your personal life, it's crucially important to become aware of and learn to proactively manage stress in your life. We're all stress managers whether we realize it or not; it's just that some methods are healthier and more effective in the long term than others. Are you alleviating the effects of stress in healthy or unhealthy ways?

Healthy ways of alleviating stress which go to the heart of the causes and don't just mask symptoms include :-

Regular alkalising exercise
Meditation and mind/body relaxation
Proper hydration
Drinking Rooibos, green tea or other no/low caffeine drinks
Healthy eating, especially plenty of green leafy vegetables and oily fish, high in omega 3
Getting the right amount of good quality sleep regularly
Yoga, Tai Chi or Pilates
Diaphragmatic breathing
Rebounding or using a trampoline
Spending time in nature
Talking through a problem with a friend
Healthy self-talk and affirmations
Laughter with friends and family
Taking regular holidays or proper breaks from work
Listening to calm or relaxing music
Reading for pleasure
Making love with your soulmate
Completing what you've started and tying up loose ends

Less healthy ways of dealing with stress which tend to simply mask the symptoms, rather than deal with underlying causes include :-

Drinking alcohol beyond moderation
Smoking
Consuming caffeinated drinks routinely
Overeating and eating unhealthily on a regular basis

Routinely burying yourself in work and neglecting other important aspects of life
Eating at your desk and not taking a proper break at lunch
Watching TV routinely for several hours a day
Taking sleeping pills
Taking long term anti-depressant or anti-anxiety medication
Distraction tactics, including immersing yourself in something to excess.

The Mind Body Connection & its Importance In Understanding Stress

In some ways, we are all chemists in our own lives because every stressful thought we think creates a chemical reaction in the brain. The brain then goes on to create a physiological reaction in the body through the release of two stress hormones I've mentioned before - cortisol and adrenaline. Conversely, the way the physical body feels and behaves under stress sends feedback to the brain and this affects our mind through our thoughts.

This helps explain why some stress-reduction techniques focus on progressive relaxation across the body which will then send soothing signals to the mind, while others such as meditation start with relaxing the mind with the aim of then sending soothing signals to the body. Both techniques work very well because of the effectiveness and power of the mind body connection. However, some people will tend to get better results from progressive relaxation across the body, while others will experience greater benefit from relaxing the mind. This is rather like having a natural preference for taking in visual, auditory, kinesthetic or digital types of information.

Once we appreciate the nature of the mind body connection, we can use it to help understand how stress is created and therefore become better equipped to deal with stress in our lives.

Therefore in order to deal with stress in the body first, try spending tem minutes relaxing every muscle group in the body one at a time, starting with the toes and slowly moving right up to the scalp. To deal with stress in the mind first, spend 15 minutes in meditation. It's easier than you think and there are plenty of free audio tracks to help get started. It only takes around 21 days to form a healthy meditation habit which can last a lifetime.

Whichever of the above two main approaches to relaxation you prefer, the impact will be felt in both your body and mind as you enter a state called homeostasis, otherwise known as self-repair. Homeostasis is the best thing you can do to deal with stress and is a powerful healing state that is not accessible through sleep alone. Prevention is so much better than cure when it comes to how to deal with stress and for this reason, it's well worth investing a little time every day in mental or physical relaxation. The benefits compound in slight edge fashion, something I'll explain in detail next.

Chapter 4 – Stress & The Slight Edge

"The single most important thing I can tell you about The Slight Edge is this: it's already working right now, either for you or against you"
Jeff Olson

The Philosophy Of The Slight Edge

Small, simple things compound to produce a massive difference. Or put even more simply "small changes, big benefits" This is the profound and powerful concept of the slight edge, named after the book "The Slight Edge: Secret To a Successful Life" by Jeff Olson. The slight edge is at work in every aspect of your life and is either taking you on an upward trajectory or a downward one. One of the best illustrations of the slight edge at work is the power of compound interest. Would you rather have a million pounds today or a penny compounded daily for the next month where the penny doubles every day? The answer to this question tells you how familiar you are with the power of the slight edge. Most people choose the million, but the penny doubled each day for 30 days compounds to over five million.

I was introduced to The Slight Edge at a breakfast networking meeting and once had I read and understood the book, realised how well it describes why we either experience great health or poor health on a daily basis. The habits and patterns that are in place in your life will either cause the slight edge to be working for or against you. Let's say that you habitually get up too late to eat a sensible breakfast and skip this vital meal on weekdays. Will this make a difference to your health and energy levels today or tomorrow? Probably not. But if this pattern continues to compound day in day out for months and years, the effects will be enormous. If you routinely skip breakfast, I predict you'll ultimately experience a variety of challenges, though these will vary from person to person. Stress, weight gain (paradoxically), low energy and libido might just name a few.

So the invisibility of the slight edge means that most people pay little or no attention to it. Watching several hours of TV each night is another example of the slight edge at work in a downwards direction. I gave away my TV when I moved house 5 years ago and it's been one of the best things I ever lost! Now I choose how I keep up with the news and what type of news I wish to pay attention to. I'm convinced that negative news coverage in slight edge fashion day in day out for years contributed to my stress and persistent low mood in 2006.

Think for a moment about how the slight edge is impacting your life and work right now. What habits and patterns are operating as forces for good or bad? Pause for a moment and make a list of your health habits, sleep habits, recreation habits, work habits, eating habits, drinking habits, intimate relationship rituals and habits with friends and family. You can't change what you're not aware of and this is a useful exercise to raise awareness.

Stress Has Massive Slight Edge Consequences

My mum died after a serious brain bleed in 2009 brought on by hypertension, but the bleed didn't occur because of one negative or stressful thought. The compounding of those stressful experiences occurred over a lifetime and resulted a dangerously high blood pressure which ultimately found her particular "crack of least resistance" in a particular blood vessel in the brain. There was an early warning sign in the form of raised blood pressure but the drugs prescribed to treat this caused her to feel sick and the doctor advised that she stop taking them. By the time the slight edge impact becomes obvious it can be too late to treat or deal with the problem, so the time to take action is now! If ever there was a compelling and logical argument that prevention is much better than cure, then the slight edge provides it.

Slight Edge Factors Compounding To Affect Stress & Work Life Balance

I've found that there are a host of stressors lurking out there, most related to poor work and lifestyle habits. When a number of these compound together, the slight edge impact can be enormous.

Isolation is a real danger and it's almost like we are hardwired for interaction and engagement. There's some truth in this because historically, primitive humans lived in communes out of a basic need for safety. When I descended into a deep depression brought on by stress in 2006, I can recall wanting to withdraw from contact with business associates, friends and family. Of course, this only served to make matters worse. Contrast this with yesterday when I met up with a small group of good friends who all do business together and help each other on a regular basis. Sitting at the lunch table, we swapped books we'd recently read, shared challenges, talked about the main things on our minds and experienced a sense of coming together that's hard to describe – almost spiritual. This is why those who are really going places often form "mastermind groups".

It's a "box life" for many in business. Go to work in a box, sit in a box all day, eat a box lunch, go home in a box and if there just happens to be time, turn on the box to be entertained at the end of the day. Unhealthy habits form so easily and the slight edge is soon at work in a downward trajectory without us realising. The box existence inevitably leads to a lack of fresh air and exercise, two factors which cause stress to build up. Being outside in nature and enjoying a favourite form of exercise on a regular basis are such great stress-busters as I've mentioned already.

Talking of the box lunch, poor eating habits especially skipping breakfast, unhealthy snacking and taking lunch at the desk, or worse still, skipping lunch, can contribute to stress, poor health and weight gain on a massive scale. It's easy to claim that the job just doesn't allow us time and scope to look after ourselves. This was the trap I fell into when working for a business psychology consultancy in Oxford. Travelling all over Europe running stressful training courses, I ate and lived very unhealthily for month after month. Half a bottle of wine every evening with a pudding after the main course seemed to make me feel temporarily less stressed. You know how easy it is to fall into this pattern. I certainly did and put on a huge amount of weight while convincing myself that there was nothing I could do about it. We may think we just don't have the time to stop for lunch, get out and get some fresh air but the truth is that productivity inevitably wanes in the afternoon. It's also vital to take regular breaks from staring at the computer. We all really know this stuff, but I keep coming back to that old Buddhist saying "to know and not to do is not yet to know".

So far, I've said little about alcohol consumption and the effects on stress and long term wellbeing. I'm not here to preach about alcohol and do still enjoy a glass of wine or beer in moderation. However using alcohol as a stress management method is hugely counterproductive. After all, alcohol is a depressant. Routinely drinking alcohol after work contributes to, rather than reduces stress in the long term. That's our old friend the slight edge at work again. Better to use more effective long-term relaxants on a regular basis, including meditation, proper hydration with wheatgrass and your favourite form of exercise. All of these will compound to move the trajectory of your life-curve upwards.

Positive Slight Edge Work Habits To Help Create A Healthy Work Life Balance

Small positive daily habits will compound to create massive benefits in just a few weeks, but only if you do them. "Do the thing and you shall have the power" as Ralph Waldo Emerson says.

Just a word about habits first. These are things that we tend to do more or less subconsciously because neural pathways have formed in the brain taking most of the activity out of conscious awareness. Think about those times when you've arrived home in the car from work and been totally unaware of the journey. That's the nature of a habit. It often only takes about 21 consecutive days of performing a simple new activity for it to start becoming a habit and is well worth the initial daily discipline.

So what simple habits can you form to help create a healthy work life balance?

1. Have the day finished on paper before it's started. Better still come up with your "success six" the evening before – the 6 key tasks you must complete the next day to move towards your goals.
2. Make sure the first thing you do at work each day is to "eat that frog" (after the book of the same name by Brian Tracy). The frog is your most important task (not necessarily the most urgent one) on your success six or to-do list.
3. Batch process emails two, or at most three times a day in order to avoid constant interruptions and to be able to focus on important tasks. Do the same with phone calls – batch them up and deal with them together if at all possible.
4. If you have to eat an elephant, the best way to do it is

one chunk at a time. In other words, break down large and seemingly intimidating tasks into bite size chunks. A good example is writing a book - 500 words a day over an 8 week period will easily generate 28,000 words. Soon, writing the 500 words a day becomes almost effortless and yet the results quickly stack up.

Can you imagine the slight edge impact on your results of combining these simple habits day after day for a year? Can you also envisage the stress-busting self-esteem that arises from such a sense of daily achievement?

Chapter 5 – It All Starts With Our Thinking

"You're only ever one thought away from feeling happy."
Michael Neill

It All starts With Thinking

If you're feeling stressed, it's your thinking that's causing that feeling. It's easy to believe that the stress is coming from something in the world "out there" but in truth, it's your thinking about what's going on that creates the stressful feelings and reactions. This was a revelation for me and very comforting because I realised that in order to feel relaxed and less stressed, I didn't have to change the world out there or wait for it to change. I just had to understand that this is the way life works.

The Illusory Nature Of The World Of Form

During several months of severe stress in 2006, I caught a powerful glimpse of the illusory nature of the world of form. Having seen it once, I became totally convinced that what we see in the world out there is much more a reflection of the quality of our thinking than anything else. The unpleasant sights, sounds and smells that I experienced while depressed were as real as any I'd ever experienced before and yet I now know for certain that they were not real. In many ways, this insight feels like a privilege and one I feel duty bound to share with others, even if at the time it was deeply frightening.

The reason I experienced those illusory negative sights, sounds and smells was because I had been thinking negative thoughts consistently for several months on end. I did the opposite of what I needed to do in order to feel happy and became depressed. It really wasn't that hard to become heavily depressed and therefore it certainly shouldn't be very hard to deal with stress and lead a happy life. This was a revelation for me and I hope it is for you too.

Every Human Being Has Innate Mental Health

Sydney Banks said this and it really resonates with me. After realising that in order to feel happy and less stressed, we just need to think better quality thoughts, the temptation is to work hard and diligently to create these types of thoughts. Paradoxically, this may well make a sense of calm and happy feelings harder, rather than easier to experience.

Coming out of hospital in 2006 was like waking up from a long nightmare. Yet I didn't need to do anything to feel massively better – I just needed to stop thinking consistently negative thoughts. I've experienced this power working in my own life. I "know" how to do this – just do nothing! The medication I was given allowed my over-active negative mind to take a break and once it could do so, I started to feel much better quite quickly.

"You Have To Bring Happiness To Life. You Don't Get Happiness Out Of Life"

These are the words of Werner Erhard and they ring true for me. Realising that "no thing" will make you happy was very liberating, rather like appreciating that when we stop searching for something, it tends to come and find us. Many business people (myself included until quite recently) have the attitude that we just have to achieve the goal and we'll be happy. The only trouble with striving for a goal to make you happy is that when you get there, a sense of "is this all there is?" can prevail. So you set another goal and the whole things starts all over again.

I started the process of becoming a Chartered Psychologist back in 1995 and remember thinking that when I achieved the goal, I'd be happy. To be honest, the journey was much more profound and powerful than the final destination arrived at 10 years later. In other words, I've found that it's really important to consciously enjoy the process of doing something which we see as contributing to the realisation of a goal. Take creating this book for example. I'm beginning to find that sitting down and writing really can be happiness-inducing in itself. Something happens in the process of writing to clarify ideas and thinking in a way that doesn't happen just by thinking about them. This in itself can make me happy if I reflect on it.

In true slight edge fashion, bringing happiness to life can become a habit – it's certainly a good one to cultivate and makes us more attractive to be around. A few simple rituals every day will compound to produce a massive difference. For example meditation, a favourite form of exercise, proper hydration, keeping in touch with loved ones and friends. These are just a few of those things that are "easy to do" but also "easy not to do", so if you don't do them today or tomorrow you probably won't feel any less happy. But over the course of a month, the positive compounding effect becomes enormous.

The Mind Body Connection Again

As already mentioned, the mind and the body are inextricably linked. Good things happening in one leads to good things happening in the other and vice versa. I can remember having a sense that I couldn't really control what went on in my mind: thoughts just seemed to "pop up" and create feelings in the body. This seems to be the way that many people operate throughout life, but I have come to appreciate that it can be very different. This is great news because no matter what happens in the external circumstances of your life, you will always be able to deal with it, once some simple truths are understood and practiced. When unhappy thoughts ran riot in my mind for months on end in early 2006, it was only a matter of time before the body started to complain.

Simple Truths To Be Aware Of And Practice

Know that whatever you are feeling at a given moment is only the product of your own thinking and no one else's. That being said, take personal responsibility for your thinking and the associated feelings created by the thinking. That way, there's no one else to blame if you don't like the results and you won't have to wait a long time for someone else to change in order for you to begin to feel better.

Pay attention to the early warning signs of stress in your own body or behaviour. Earlier, I encouraged you to think about how manifests for you. It's much easier to interrupt a limiting pattern around stress creation when you can spot the early warning signs. Most importantly, take constructive action by choosing something from the list of positive stress-busters.

If your mind is feeling agitated, you probably won't make great decisions and certainly won't be open to the power of effective intuition which relies on connecting with universal intelligence. Think of the cluttered and agitated mind as creating static around the reception of effective and clear thinking. Use meditation and other forms of relaxation to clear the static and feel better.

Chapter 6 – Happy Pills Don't Make You Happy Or Deal With Stress

"Happiness is not something ready made. It comes from your own actions"
The Dalai Lama

Happiness And Its Relationship To Stress And Work Life Balance

Have you noticed that feelings of happiness and negative stress are mutually exclusive i.e. that we can't experience them both at the same time?. We can be happy and stressed waiting to give a presentation but the feelings in the body and mind will be very different compared to if we were feeling unhappy and stressed. Feelings of happiness seem to make the stress very manageable and relatively short lived. Perhaps the difference is the extent to which we feel in control of the situation and our response to it. This is where work life balance becomes important: when our lives are in balance, we have greater feelings of control and therefore stress seems much more manageable.

Anti-Depressants Mask The Symptoms And Don't Deal With Underlying Causes Of Stress

If you experience depression or anxiety and visit the doctor, there is a strong chance that some form of medication will be prescribed. The challenge for doctors is that appointments are rarely more than ten minutes and in such a short period of time, it's very difficult to make more than a cursory diagnosis of the real problem. When I visited one of the GPs at my local surgery after experiencing prolonged stress symptoms in early 2006, I was asked "apart from writing you out a cheque for £80,000 what would you like me to do?" This wasn't a frivolous question; the doctor was effectively acknowledging his inability (quite rightly) to help deal with the underlying causes of my depression. Of course, it was my choice how to interpret the perceived financial loss I was beating myself up for. Choosing to interpret it as a big investment in my financial education would have been much more constructive.

Unfortunately, I visited the doctor that day with very unrealistic expectations of what could be done to help me. I wanted to feel better fast and so a strange type of collaborative conspiracy emerged whereby the doctor prescribed something which I in turn believe would alleviate the problems I was experiencing. In this particular case, I was prescribed a sleeping tablet called Zopiclone because I told the doctor that my biggest problem was not being able to sleep. Having difficulty sleeping was of course a side effect of chronic stress and what I really needed to do was go to work on the underlying causes of that stress by thinking better thoughts. But a ten minute appointment provided no real possibility of doing so or better still, teaching me the relevant life skills.

Any drug that might have been prescribed that day could do no more than mask the symptoms I was experiencing without addressing the underlying causes. I saw three different GPs within the space of a few weeks and all followed the same type of approach. Unfortunately, it was too late to put preventative measures in place and what I needed was immediate and remedial help. This is the only basis on which I believe drugs can be prescribed and then other longer term measures are required in addition. Drugs would not help me change the negative thinking patterns and lifestyle habits which had created the problems I was experiencing. With professional help, I needed to fundamentally reappraise what was going on in my life, having lost touch with what was most important – my loved ones, family and friends. One of my main aims in writing this book is to give you the tools and techniques to change the type of negative thinking patterns and poor lifestyle habits that contribute inch by inch to chronic stress.

Anti-Depressants Don't Work Straight Away

The problem with presenting myself at the doctors and looking for an immediate way to feel better was that it takes at least 3 weeks for anti-depressant medication to have any effect if it does so at all. The first drug I was prescribed (Citalopram 20mg, also known as Prozac) had absolutely no effect at all for me after more than 3 weeks. This disappointment came on the back of the knowledge that it had made a significant difference for a relative who was taking the drug long-term. I'm not going to delve in the detail of how these drugs are supposed to work because it's well documented elsewhere. However, the theory is that drugs like Citalopram gradually alter the chemical balance of the brain, allowing the patient to begin to feel better and get to work on improving other aspects of their life.

The problem is that anti-depressant drugs don't work in the same way for everyone and they have different side effects for different people. This strikes me as highly risky, especially as I discovered from my own experience that very effective natural alternatives are available in the form of high quality fish oil and evening primrose oil. I also tried St John's Wort but found that it seemed to make my heart race or perhaps that was just a placebo type of effect.

Chapter 7 – Healthy Work Life Balance & Its Relationship To Stress

"A Situation In Which You Are Able To Give The Right Amount Of Time And Effort To Your Work And To Your Personal Life Outside Work"
The Financial Times

Salient Elements Of Work Life Balance

The Financial Times' definition of work life balance makes some important points. Firstly, it describes a situation, rather than a more permanent state of affairs and one which will be unique and different for everyone, based on their own circumstances. Secondly, it alludes to the individual having an element of control over the situation by referring to the ability to give the right amount of time and effort to work and personal life. Feeling that we have an element of control over the circumstances of our life is a key determinant of whether or not we will feel the negative effects of stress.

The reality is that we can always feel in control because we can consciously influence what we think and therefore how we feel as described in the previous chapter. It's easy to fall into the trap of thinking that we have a mortgage to pay or a family to raise and this means that we have to work and live life in a particular way.

How Do You Know If Work And Life Are In Balance?

Feelings of negative stress are less prevalent and less likely to occur when work and life are in balance. This is effectively your own personal feedback mechanism for achieving balance but it's not entirely reliable because what might seem like a reasonable work life balance for one person may not seem like it to another. It's something to do with the boundary that we create between life and work and everyone constructs and puts this boundary in their own unique place. Work life balance certainly does not mean allocating an equal amount of time and effort to work and activities outside of work. Optimal work life balance will vary over time, depending on your specific work and life circumstances. The key question to ask yourself is "does my current work life balance situation create feelings of happiness?" If it does, then the chances are you are enjoying a semblance of balance.

Feedback from others is important too, particularly from work colleagues, family and friends. If your current situation is having a detrimental effect on relationships with colleagues, family or friends then it's likely that work and life are not in balance.

It can help to consider 4 key life quadrants in relation to work and life before examining how well these are balanced for you:

1. Work
2. Family
3. Friends
4. Self

Consider how much time and effort is expended on each. As mentioned above, it won't be an equal split but needs to feel appropriate and that you are in control of the time and effort expended in the 4 life quadrants. In the same way that a feeling of being in control is a key determinant of whether we experience negative stress, a sense of being in control is the psychology of creating what feels like a healthy work life balance. The key word here is psychology because life clearly has an unpredictable element for us all; it's how we handle the uncertainty that makes the difference.

So I'm Definitely Feeling Out Of Balance, What Now?

Firstly, recognise that it's a useful feeling and not something to feel threatened by. The feeling caused by your thinking is a valuable opportunity to take stock and consider the implications. Here are some practical tips and suggestions to help you :-

1. Establish boundaries and be explicit about these with other important stakeholders e.g. family, close friends, work colleagues and clients. Having established these boundaries, stick to them and monitor the impact
2. Aligned to the first suggestion is the need to schedule and spend regular time with close family and friends. For example, the practice of spending a "date night" with a partner once a week is a well established one and can work well
3. Take regular exercise. As I've said already, there are so many benefits of regular exercise, including better sleep pattern, increased stress threshold, less irritability, better brain functioning and problem solving because of an increased oxygen supply to the brain, feelings of youthfulness and vitality, better overall health, increased immunity from minor and major illness. The list goes on and on. Find a form that works for you, schedule it for 21 consecutive days and you'll become addicted to the benefits – in a healthy and positive way.
4. Look for and implement ways of mentally switching off. Burn out is the result of trying to do too much for too long without providing opportunities for mental rest and relaxation. The problem with burn out is that you'll be forced to rest and relax, so much better to watch for the early warning signs, such as waking early on a regular basis, increased irritability and chronic stress symptoms. My favourite way of mentally switching off is through the practice of regular meditation and I'll say much more about this later. A walk in nature, time spent on a

favourite hobby and a weekend away are examples of other ways in which you might mentally switch off

5. Look for ways to work smarter, rather than harder. Anyone can be a busy fool. Are you addressing the things that really need to be addressed, outsourcing or delegating things you could, saying "no" when you really should, allowing you to say "yes" to the things that really matter
6. Make sure that you take regular short breaks, especially when working in front of a computer screen. Make time for lunch away from the work environment whenever possible
7. Get things into perspective by using a technique called reframing. What are the positives arising from this situation? (they're always there if you look for them). Talk through the situation with a mentor or coach for added perspective
8. Think back and remind yourself why you're working in the way you are. Are the drivers and rationale still valid and important? It may be time to make a change and moving away from pain is a powerful motivational force, so don't ignore it.
9. Come up with your own definition of a successful life in each of the 4 quadrants above. Give some thought to this and consider how your current situation maps across.

Chapter 8 – Resilience Is The New Work Life Balance Requirement

What Is Resilience?

The best definition I've come across is from business psychologists Robertson Cooper "The capacity to maintain a high level of performance and positive well being in the face of challenges".

While a certain level of challenge is energising and motivating, rather like stress, once the level of challenge that we are facing goes beyond our perceived ability to cope, we can become dysfunctional. By dysfunctional, I mean that performance drops off and we begin to feel that life is somehow out of control. Everyone has a different resilience threshold but there is plenty we can do to raise our personal threshold. Robertson Cooper outline four core components of resilience and by working on each of these, we can significantly enhance our resilience

1. Confidence
2. Social support
3. Adaptability
4. Purposefulness

When we feel confident and in control, problems seem much more manageable and we can often cut through them like a knife through butter. Without confidence we struggle. So what exactly is confidence and why does it matter? Confidence could be defined as faith in our own ability to make the things we want to happen actually happen. When we feel confident, we also feel competent and effective in our ability to cope with stressful situations. Strong self esteem also goes hand in hand with confidence; a sense of liking oneself and having a positive self-image. I'll say much more about the power of a positive self image later, in the chapter titled "building self esteem and self confidence".

Social support is vital for all of us. Babies can die from something called "failure to thrive syndrome", otherwise known as a lack of love. As adults, we also need the love and support of others close to us in order to deal with the adverse situations that life brings, rather than just trying to cope on our own. Think about a time when you coped with a significant challenge and the role that social support played in the coping strategy. Just knowing that others care seems to give us greater fortitude and strength. Therefore it's crucially important to nurture our close relationships, both family and friends. I'll go into much more depth on this in a later chapter - "cherish your connections".

By adaptability, I mean the flexibility to adapt to situations which are beyond our control and this is an essential component to building and maintaining resilience. In particular, resilience enables us to cope well with change and our recovery from the impact of change tends to be quicker. Knowing that "whatever happens, I'll be able to handle it" is a powerful way to live. When I discovered that my life savings had been stolen by a fraudster, I had to quickly adapt and come up with new ways of paying for my sons' education. What I discovered was that adaptability goes hand in hand with the other three core components of resilience. Confidence, social support and a clear sense of purpose all helped me to find creative and practical solutions to the problem.

Purposefulness could be defined in this context as having a clear sense of purpose, together with clear values, drive and direction. When we have these things, we're able to be much more persistent and achievement orientated in the face of setbacks. Therefore a clear sense of purpose is the fuel to propel ourselves through the inevitable setbacks and disappointments that come up both in our business and personal lives. Once I discovered a clear sense of purpose which went beyond just making money, everything began to change. I'll say much more about this in a later chapter titled "finding your purpose". In short, when the why is powerful enough, the how becomes easy.

By building and enhancing our resilience, we become more than we were before. This is a powerful way of reframing problems and challenges because they make us grow and become a better person. Instead of fearing problems, we can use them as stepping stones to a better life and this has never been more true than in the area of work life balance. If work seems to be outbalancing life, how can the four components of resilience help you bring it back into line?

Chapter 9 – Health, Stress & Work Life Balance

"Health Is The First Wealth."
Anthony Robbins

Your Health Equals The Sum Of Your Habits

The second chapter of this book shows you how to get fit for business and life in just 12 weeks. The simple steps outlined there can easily become healthy habits. In typical slight edge fashion, these are easy to do and also easy not to do. It's your choice.

The main challenge in creating great health is that it rarely becomes a significant priority until we have a major problem. By this stage, we're probably dealing with cure rather than prevention. Unfortunately, cure tends to be much more expensive and far less reliable as a long term health strategy and that's as long as the damage is reversible. How many business leaders find that they've mortgaged their health after their mid-50s and can't get it back again?

Health & Energy Are Everything In Business

There's a massive difference between feeling ok some of the time and feeling totally healthy and energetic most of the time. Getting up every day feeling on top of your game and eager to get going is a fantastic feeling and living with abundant energy positively impacts every area of life. Enhanced libido, looking great, stress tolerance, virtual immunity from the minor bugs like colds and stomach upsets, as well as reduced risk of contracting a major life-threatening illness. Rather than wait until problems hit, invest a little time each day in your health and this will pay massive dividends. Feeling physically and mentally strong allows you to play a much higher game. If you think that sounds like hard work, you should try feeling crappy most of the time – now that's hard work!

Ageing Doesn't Have To Be Painful & Unhealthy

I meet many people in business who assume that being a few stone overweight, having ailments and taking a day or two off for colds and flu' every few months is just part of life. What my health crash did was give me the incentive to research and put into practice some highly effective daily habits which have not only given me immunity from depression but also provide a level of energy and wellbeing which feels little short of miraculous. Hitting bottom was probably the best thing that could have happened because the only way left was up. Many people never hit bottom, so continue to go deeper without realising they are in significant trouble until disaster strikes "out of the blue".

I don't know about you but I would much prefer to live a long and healthy life where ailments and illness are not a perpetual challenge which gets tougher and tougher as life goes on. Old age really doesn't need to be painful and riddled with ailments and illness.

Healthy Slight Edge Habits To Help Deal With Stress

You know from chapter two that omega 3 oils are good for you and especially for the brain. The brain is composed of 75-80% fat and to keep it in peak condition and deal with stress efficiently, it's important to feed the brain the right fats. Omega 3 is particularly found in oily fish, walnuts and olive oil. Omega 3 oils are an effective antidepressant and mood enhancer without the unpleasant side effects. It's easy to get into the habit of drizzling extra virgin olive oil over your salad or adding some walnuts which contain six times more omega 3 than other nuts.

Rebounding or bouncing on a trampoline is probably the best way of getting the lymph system moving. The lymph system is in effect the body's sewage system for the removal of toxins, but unlike the circulatory system there's a design flaw here. We don't have the equivalent of a heart to provide a pumping function for the lymph system, so it benefits from some external stimulation. Rebounding for a few minutes a day will get both the heart and the lymph system moving; it provides an excellent daily detox and is a great stress-buster.

In the same way that rebounding is a good way of removing toxins from the body, a stress massage from an expert can also be highly effective. Lactic acid can easily build up, especially in the area of the shoulders and neck. Has anyone ever massaged your shoulders or neck and pointed out knots in the tissue? These knots are small stores of lactic acid. We often sit in the same position in front of a computer or the wheel of a car for hours at a time under stress and without proper relaxation breaks. This can cause muscle stiffness and discomfort as a result of lactic acid build up.

Incompletions are a potential source of stress; tasks or things we know we should do and which either have not been started yet or have been started and left unfinished. Things we haven't completed take up valuable mental capacity and occupy the subconscious mind. They are out of conscious awareness but they act as a brake on wellbeing and optimal productivity. Make a list of your current incompletions, be they things to do around the house or tasks you've been putting off at work and then fully complete them, focusing on one at a time as you gradually tick them off the list.

Aligned to incompletions is indecision and it's a significant stressor for many people in business. Being undecided about whether to stay in a relationship, change jobs, find a new career, start or make a success of your own business are examples of situations in which commitment will be lacking. Some days you feel like going one way, some days another and this is a huge psychic drain on energy levels as the subconscious mind runs riot trying to resolve the dilemma. I'm a big fan of the "no lose" model of decision making. A committed decision means cutting oneself off from any other possibility and aligning thoughts, words and actions behind the decision. If make you make the wrong decision, you can change it later, but just make a decision and know that it will all work out in the end. Try this with a decision you've been putting off.

The Best Time To Start Is Now

My complete 12 week formula for feeling totally energetic, healthy and vibrant is explained in chapter 2. If you've not already begun, don't wait another day to start to put this great information into practice. The sooner you start, the sooner you'll be experiencing the benefits in all areas of life and work.

Chapter 10 – Running Your Brain For Resilience

"Life will give you whatever experience is the most helpful for the evolution of your consciousness"
Eckhart Tolle

The Power Of Beliefs And Creating Supportive Beliefs

The quotation which starts this chapter makes for a very powerful belief. If we regard whatever happens to us in life as ultimately helpful for the evolution of our consciousness, then nothing can really ever go wrong. I know that might sound a little far-fetched but it's a fair point; life tends to turn out pretty much in line with the beliefs we have about life. The challenge is that very often those beliefs are held in the subconscious mind and are not accessible to us. Consequently, life just seems to happen around us.

Here are a few healthy and supportive beliefs about life :-
Love is everywhere
I am loving and I am loveable
I love myself just the way I am
I love and approve of myself
All is perfect, all is well
I am peaceful with all of my emotions
I trust the process of life to bring me my highest good
Life supports me. I am passionate about life
I have unlimited potential
I see my goals through to completion: I am a highly successful
I am strong, healthy and energetic every day
I have a really great body
I trust my inner wisdom
I express gratitude for all the good in my life
I look for things to appreciate everywhere

Every day brings wonderful new surprises
I dissolve resentment
I am willing to forgive myself and others
I forgive and I set myself free

Notice your reaction to the list...Do some or all of these statements line up with your beliefs about life or do the statements seems false and ill-fitting? Some of these statements are from Louise Hay's excellent book "You Can Heal Your Life". Louise Hay recommends standing in front of a mirror twice a day and reading your own affirming life statements with passion and feeling. The first few times you do this, it might seem a little odd but the benefits start to come as the words start to re-programme the subconscious mind through daily repetition. Once that starts to happen, you'll begin to feel happier and create better results in all areas of life. This is another powerful example of the slight edge at work. Many of us programmed our subconscious minds for unhappiness in a slight edge way through repeated negative thinking earlier in life. You can turn this around by daily repetition of positive, life-affirming statements.

Look At What's Going On In Your Life For Evidence Of Your Beliefs

We tend to get back what we put out into life, be that thoughts or actions. So if you want to know the quality of your current beliefs, simply take a look at the outcomes you are currently experiencing in life. I remember reading something similar about beliefs around 10 years ago and thinking that it all seemed like a "black box" and that there was no way I could access and change my beliefs. With some simple daily practices like meditation, positive visualisation and affirmations, there has been a huge shift in beliefs. Perhaps the most important one you can work on is to learn to love and approve of yourself. Psychologists have found that "positive self-regard" is **the** major component of emotional intelligence – the ability to handle the emotional side of life in a positive and constructive way. I'm not talking about arrogance – this arises from feelings of inferiority. It's healthy positive self-esteem that will see you through the challenges life brings and enable you to come out wiser and richer for the experience.

The World Is Your Mirror

I came across this concept in the Deepak Chopra meditation series on relationships and it really got me thinking. The proposition is that everything we see, feel and experience in life is a reflection of who we are. The power in this viewpoint is that if we don't like something that is going on in our lives, all we need to do is take responsibility for what's in the mirror and look within. Instead of staying stuck by blaming outside circumstances or worse still, running away from the situation, we can feel empowered to change things. This really resonates with me in the context of relationships because I have found that I only properly learn about relationships by being in one ! Focusing on gratitude for the good things I have in the relationship shifts the view that I see in the mirror and replaces feelings like frustration and anger with feelings of love and genuine appreciation. Make a list of twenty things you really love and appreciate about your partner next time you're feeling frustrated or angry with them. This simple exercise really shifts feelings fast and will enable you to feel much more resourceful instead of feeling stuck. When our thinking is coming from ego, we tend to feel stressed, make poor decisions and take unsuitable actions. When thinking comes from love and compassion, we feel good and are much more likely to take positive, effective actions.

Meditation Can Be Miraculous

If there's one thing that's made the greatest difference in my ability to handle stress and pressure, it's daily meditation. I first became exposed to meditation when working in the corporate world and during a period of feeling exhausted and stressed, responded to an advertisement to learn Transcendental Meditation (TM) in The Sunday Times newspaper. The advert described a few of the benefits of regular meditation – better sleep pattern, greater clarity of thinking and reduced stress. I paid £400 and attended a small number of 1:1 coaching sessions with a TM teacher. The mechanics of meditation were explained and I was given a mantra to repeat mentally. In the case of TM mantras are specific Sanskrit words or phrases which have a spiritual meaning. An advantage of using such a word is that it doesn't tend to create any extra thought patterns in your mind which could cause the brain to wander off away from the mental silence.

The initial challenge I had with this form of meditation was that my mind wanted to go everywhere but remain on the mantra. This is very common and was explained as symptomatic of something akin to a mental detox. In other words, it's important not to fight the extraneous thoughts and to bring the mind gently back to silently repeating the mantra. Most people experience this "monkey mind" which can't stay still when they start meditation and many give up the practice because benefits don't seem to appear quickly enough. I practised TM quite religiously for about 12 months and this involved sitting in silence and mentally repeating the Sanskrit mantra for 20 minutes, twice a day.

After about a month, I definitely began to sleep better and experience less stress. Spurred on by these benefits, I persisted with the meditation practice. After about 12 months and feeling much less stressed, I gradually stopped daily meditation practice and this turned out to be a mistake. The benefits of meditation accrue in typical "slight edge" fashion and this can create the sense that nothing much is happening and it doesn't really matter whether the daily practice is continued or not. I've come to appreciate that it makes a massive difference. Daily meditation seems to provide an inoculation effect against the effects of stress.

Finding it difficult to make the time to practice TM twice daily for 20 minutes, I looked for other less time-consuming methods. I used an audio programme called Holosync for a few months, although found it quite expensive and there is a well-marketed upgrade path. After moving to the second level with Holosync when my own affirmations were subliminally recorded on the underlying track, I felt it wasn't very beneficial and stopped practicing the method.

Another meditation system that I do recommend is a series of audio tracks called "Into The Vortex" by Esther and Gerry Hicks. The CD and accompanying book comprises 4 different 15 minute meditations in the areas of general wellbeing, financial abundance, health and relationships.

The system that I now use daily and really enjoy is the meditation series by Dr Deepak Chopra. This classically trained medical practitioner was introduced to TM and has gone on to study Ayurvedic medicine and meditation practices in great depth. The beauty of Deepak Chopra's meditations is that they last for just 15 minutes each and are a series of well-guided audios. I've found that after practicing this method of meditation for the last 6 months every day, my mind wanders far less and is able to remain silent or focused on the mantra. It's the silent mind that allows the mind and body to remove into what Deepak Chopra terms "homeostasis" or self repair. He describes this as the best thing you can do and some claim that daily meditation over a period of many years can actually reverse the effects of ageing. You can listen to an excellent example of these meditations which includes an explanation of homeostasis and the mind-body connection. Please visit www.AndrewBridgewater.com/relaxation

It's difficult to convince anyone of the amazing benefits of mediation until they begin to experience these in mind and body. Those of my clients who go on to practice daily meditation experience far higher levels of success through my coaching that those that don't persist with this simple daily habit. Perhaps the most significant benefit and yet also the least tangible is an increased ability to handle whatever comes up in life with a positive "can-do" attitude. Anything can happen to you, the important thing is what you choose to do with what happens.

A final piece of advice on meditation – you don't have to be perfect to gain the benefits. The same goes for all the simple health practices outlined here. In the case of meditation, sometimes the mind will wander everywhere but on the mantra and it feels as though there's little benefit gained at the end of 15 minutes. Meditation is a process which delivers benefits from daily repetition and sometimes the repetition feels blissful and utterly peaceful while sometimes it doesn't. The benefits will accrue whichever way it feels and I simply urge anyone reading this to make it a habit and then watch their life change for the better. You be the judge.

Avoid Ruminating On A Problem For More Than 10 Minutes At A Time

I first came across this technique in a book called "The Depression Cure" by Dr Steve Ilardi. Ruminating is what cows do when chewing on grass and if you watch them, you'll notice that they ruminate for literally hours at a time. How often have you done that with a problem? I know I have and according to Dr Ilardi, diminishing returns start to set in after around 10 minutes, so we need to move on and think about something else. Very often when we move the thinking on, a possible solution or way forward with the problem will pop into the mind when you are least expecting it – in the shower just after applying shampoo for example! The idea is similar to the principle of "sleeping on something" without making a decision. The subconscious mind, freed up from the background noise and stress created by excess ruminating will usually come up with a solution on its own.

Forgiveness Is A Powerful Resilience Booster

One of the best definitions of forgiveness I've come across is "letting go of the hope that the past could have been any different". When we genuinely forgive ourselves and others, we complete the past, rather like ticking off a significant item on our personal list of incompletions! Pick a simple example from your own life. The head teacher who said you'd never amount to anything, the ex-partner who never paid you back the money you lent them in good faith, the person who defrauded you. These are all items from my personal forgiveness list and I feel so much better by forgiving and letting go of the pain and resentment.

The Power Of Daily Gratitude

An attitude of gratitude is one of the best ways to feel genuinely happy and is a great stress-buster. Gratitude is like a muscle – the more you use it, the better it gets. Also, the more we are grateful for all the good things in our lives, the more good things we tend to have to be grateful for.

There are many ways of embedding an attitude of gratitude into your life and my favourites are the daily gratitude journal and "daily magic". Starting a gratitude journal simply involves buying a nicely bound journal (leather works well) and spending 10 minutes each evening before bed writing down what you're grateful for that day. After a few weeks, a new habit forms and a growing sense of peace and gratitude starts to pervade life, something that's very attractive to be around.

"Daily magic" is a set of simple rituals described by Anthony Robbins as a great way to start each day. It starts with 3 minutes of a simple breathing pattern whilst walking of 4 sharp breaths in through the nose followed by 4 sharp breaths out through the mouth. Then speaking out loud all the things you are grateful for in life for 3 minutes. "I'm so grateful for my two wonderful sons, I'm so grateful for the love I share with my partner, I'm so grateful for the wide open fields at the bottom of the garden and the peace and tranquility they bring into my life, I'm so grateful for being able to write this book and share my ideas and inspiration with the world..." Then spend anything from 15 to 45 minutes doing your favourite form of exercise whilst using powerful incantations out loud. The list at the beginning of this chapter will do beautifully.

The reason "daily magic" works its magic is that daily repetition with feelings of positive thoughts and statements literally re-programmes the subconscious mind. More classic "slight edge" stuff and again these are easy to do and easy not to do. It's your choice.

Visualisation Has Been Described As The Great Secret Of Success

One of the components of "Daily Magic" described above is the visualisation of goals. All of us visualise whether we realise it or not. The question is are you visualising what you want to create in life or what you don't want to create? The brain can't deal with negation which is why if I say "don't think of a pink elephant", the first thing you think about is a pink elephant.

I have to admit that I don't find it easy to see things clearly in my mind. However, I can feel the effect of something I think about and this is a form of visualisation. Whether you are a more visual or kinesthetic person, it doesn't matter; you can still enjoy the benefits of visualisation. It's another slight edge technique that benefits from regular repetition which is why Tony Robbins advocates making visualisation part of your daily routine. It's simply a matter of imagining or feeling (or preferably both) what you want to create in life. Rather like during meditation, the mind tends to wander off topic. As for meditation, bring the mind gently back to what you want to create, seeing and feeling the results you want. I do know this works, because I did it in reverse through visualising and feeling highly negative things; it only took 4 months of daily repetition for me to end up in a very dark place!

Maximising Your Chances Of Being Resilient By Choosing The Right Opportunities

Resilience is a popular word in the corporate world, especially in the content of change and the ability to manage and live with change. I've learned some powerful lessons here since taking up a full time job in May 2014.

I joined a relatively small psychometric test publishing business that had just been acquired by a global HR management consultancy. I'd done some work as an associate with the test publisher for about 2 years and liked the people and the way the business operated. So there was already some two-way awareness and understanding or how both I and the business worked together. This was a big deal for me, because the thought of entering back in the world of full-time employment was a significant decision and needed exactly the right fit of opportunity meeting talents.

The first job offer I received was from a training business in which I'd be required to deliver training up to 5 days a week, in addition to designing new training offerings and managing other people. As part of the pre-offer negotiations, I asked if I could deliver training for a maximum of 4 days a week on average, to allow quality time to be put into other key components of the role. This was met with a definitive "not possible" with the explanation that it would create a difficult precedent in relation to other staff who were routinely required to train 5 days a week. It was not a difficult decision to decline the company's offer of a job, despite the good salary and benefits package. I would probably burn out in 6 months to a year and indeed, it transpired that other people had recently left the business for similar reasons. So a key learning here is to make the right choice of job in order to maximize your chances of dealing with stress and creating a healthy work-life balance in the first place. Some opportunities will signpost challenges immediately and it's important to trust your intuition here as well as clarify facts such as:-

- How much travel is necessary and how much time would I be spending working away from home?
- What have people tended to say when they left the company (both positive and less positive)?
- What sort of working pattern does my potential boss follow? Are they a 70 hour a week person or more balanced in the way they like to work? Whatever they might say to the contrary, a boss who works very excessive hours is likely to expect this of others too.
- Am I required to commit significant time and effort to accountabilities which are likely to have to be fulfilled outside normal working hours?
- Is there any potential to work from home at certain times in order to reduce commuting and increase productivity when needing to focus on key tasks?

After receiving 3 offers of employment, I joined the psychometric test publisher at the start of May 2014 and quickly became involved in running psychometric test training as well as selling and conducting consultancy assignments. It was varied and interesting work which often involving visiting clients' premises and there was some travel required too. But neither requirement was excessive. The opportunity also seemed to "feel right" and broadly answered the above questions positively.

Two years in, I have a demanding job but have managed stress well and maintain a good work life balance.

Chapter 11 – Finding Your Purpose

"The two most important days in your life are the day you are born and the day you find out why."
Mark Twain

Why Do You Work?

I know there's an obvious answer but just ponder the question for a moment. After the mortgage, the bills, the holidays, the car, the necessities of life have been paid, why do you really work? If your answer isn't something like "because I really love what I do", then it's time to think seriously about making some changes. This isn't a career change handbook but I do want to provide some insights from my own experience of having wrestled with the whole "why work?" question.

For many years, I struggled to find what I loved to do and only found it after much trial and error. I found that being a trainee chartered accountant was a very unfulfilling way to work. That's not to say there won't be people reading this who find the profession fascinating but I just didn't have the right skills and ways of thinking. I can remember feeling a complete failure that day I drafted my resignation letter to the staff partner at Grant Thornton. I didn't have another job to go to or even any idea of what sort of job I might look for. I just knew that I have to break the vicious circle and get out fast. When you do that, things often get worse before they get better – and they did!

One of the advantages I saw in applying for graduate traineeships was that I didn't necessarily need to commit to a vocation without really knowing anything about it. Bass considered me for roles in both marketing and IT when I was successful at their 2 day graduate assessment centre. Strangely, after what's written above, I joined them in June, 3 months before the rest of the graduate intake in September to help out with some spreadsheet work in the management accounts department. I'd actually enjoyed working with a package called Lotus 123 after spending 3 days being trained in it by Grant Thornton at Bradenham Manor in Buckinghamshire.

I finally joined the systems department at Cape Hill Brewery in Birmingham in October 1986 after spending several weeks in a variety of what I can only describe as fascinating familiarisation of some of the key areas of the brewing industry. We had to run a pub for a fortnight and I spent 2 weeks getting up at 4.30am to go out on deliveries with the draymen in Burton on Trent, a long drive from Selly Oak in Birmingham where I was living. Manhandling a full 36 gallon barrel down a cellar staircase is something I'll never forget. The pub I ran was in Marston Green, Birmingham just half a mile from my first school and the biggest challenge was dealing with Marston Green's unruly and inebriated customers on a Friday night. Also, I never appreciated how much effort and time goes in to producing a fine pint of cask-conditioned ale until I had to do it. Get the process wrong and the whole barrel is ruined.

I was very fortunate to be given a dream project towards the end of my first year in the systems department at Cape Hill. The brewery was setting up a pilot health club and gym at a run-down old city boozer at Parsons Green, Birmingham. It was a radical move for the company and I was asked to organise and implement the IT, administration systems and procedures at what came to be known as "Gymtrac At The Sporting Parson". There are times in life when we seem to get a lucky break and this was a big one for me, coming just a year after the heartache of resigning a job without another to go to. I had however capably delivered some smaller projects on time and within budget in the first year at Bass, which presumably convinced Mike Lowe, systems manager that I was a "safe pair of hands" and he decided to put the Gymtrac project my way. I vividly recall being asked to go into Mike's office where he asked how

I felt about being involved in something which was new and quite high risk for the company. I jumped at the opportunity enthusiastically as I loved the whole Gymtrac concept with a passion and felt excited to be working on something so new and different which involved much more than following a existing blueprint. I researched membership packages, electronic point of sale systems (when they were still very new), made recommendations and then implemented those in a very tight time scale to enable Gymtrac to open on time and within budget. I'm sure the success of this project was instrumental in me securing a prestigious job with Deloitte Haskins & Sells Management Consultancy Division in Manchester a year later.

The reason I've elaborated on the Gymtrac project is that it was one of those times when I'd have worked for free because I loved it so much. It was the combination of project management and being asked to run a ground-breaking initiative where there were many unknowns. Given a challenge of that type, I tend to rise to it and Gymtrac became the first of several in my career. Perhaps the biggest of all was the decision to retrain as a chartered psychologist.

That Mid-Life Moment

I love Carl Jung's views on mid-life. Jung was a Swiss psychiatrist and psychologist whose theories of personality gave rise to a vast body of knowledge, including the Myers Briggs Type Indicator (MBTI) which I spent 2 years training practitioners how to use when working for OPP in Oxford. According to Jung, when we reach mid-life (and he never defined exactly when that was), we seek to explore and develop the opposite sides of our personality. I'm simplifying things here and anyone who is familiar with psychological type will immediately realise this. However, I think the elegance of Jung's ideas lies in their simplicity when boiled right down to the core.

Many people reading this will be able to identify with that sense of "is this all there is?" Have I worked so long and hard up until now just to experience these frustrations, this lack of fulfillment, these crazy hours, this much unrelenting pressure and stress? Do I really want the remainder of my career to comprise more of the same? Or perhaps I can reinvent myself, spending the rest of life doing something profound, powerful and very purposeful? After all, I've only got one life (let's not debate that one as it's a whole new book!).

Time is the only finite resource in our lives - think about it for a moment. You can earn more money, experience more love, be happier and more fulfilled but you can't get any more time. When the game's up, it's over. Therefore, after appreciating that time really is the only limited resource, we want to start using it more wisely and investing it more purposefully. We begin to think about the legacy of our lives and want the quality of the time we have left to be better. To arrive at this realisation is a great gift because from then on, life becomes a game where we are playing with the house's money. In other words, we can't lose when we become true to ourselves and what really matters to us. The beauty of the game is that these things are different for everyone, so we're not competing with others for finite and limited resources.

So when you get home from work one night, feeling utterly dejected, stressed, frustrated and fed up – it's a gift. Perhaps this is your personal tipping point when things start to be re-evaluated and re-prioritised with the intention of being able to live out life's true purpose with passion.

I can recall reaching such a point whilst working for a large management consulting firm. The feeling of kudos on joining from Bass 5 years earlier had been amazing, the pay excellent and the work varied and often interesting but after a couple of years, I had a growing and uneasy feeling that I was just a pawn in someone else's big chess game that I had no control over, to be moved and sometimes captured at will. That particular night, I was sharing a hotel room in London with my brother Peter. As it happened, we were both working for the same consulting organisation after the merger of two legacy firms a year earlier. Peter had originally joined one and I had joined the other, though we operated in different specialist areas.

One of us said something like " how long are we going to keep doing this ?" and then the floodgates opened and it all started to pour out – that stacked up series of resistances and resentments which once the pile reaches the ceiling and you can't see over it, creates a wall of frustration. Something happened to me that night and I vowed to make some changes. I didn't know how or what the end result would look like, I just knew things had to change. I've learned to welcome those points in life because they create movement and momentum for change. Ten years later I had found a whole new career as a chartered psychologist.

Considering Making A Living Without A Job?

One of the biggest dilemmas faced by leaders is "should I work in a job or could I make it out there on my own"? If you've never been very good at the big corporate game, you may find it very difficult to follow ways of working that seem slightly inefficient and political. That being said, the predictable monthly salary, company car, health insurance and pension scheme are very helpful.

The best piece of advice I can offer anyone who is contemplating self-employment is to thoroughly understand your personal preferences on a continuum which has variety/risk at one end and certainty at the other. How much do you need certainty from month to month and how much do you need risk and variety? The reality is that many self-employed professionals regard themselves as having more security than their employed colleagues, mainly because as a self-employed person you are truly in control. No boss or HR manager can call you into the office one day and say that your role has been made redundant. This represents something of a shift in mindset for many and will often only occur after a few years of successful self-employment. The other thing is that you do need to be comfortable with selling yourself, be that to other consultancies who buy in your services or directly to clients.

Max Comfort wrote an useful book entitled 'Portfolio People: How To Create A Work Lifestyle As Individual As You Are' back in the late 1990s. I'd urge anyone contemplating moving from the ranks of the employed to the self-employed world to check out the book for more hints and tips.

How I Found Purpose In Work

Each of us will find a unique route to our purpose but I thought it would be useful to share mine as an example. To be clear, it's not been a perfect linear upward path; there have been numerous dips and challenges along the way. Back in 1994, my then wife Sue and I decided that as professionals in our mid 30s, we'd both been working too hard for too long without a proper holiday. I was feeling burnt out in corporate life after spending 18 months working away from home as project manager for Mercury Communications, who at that time were the only competitor to BT in the UK Telecoms market. I was literally exhausted and starting to feel quite stressed which is why I investigated and became trained in Transcendental Meditation (TM).

Sue and I decided to purchase a round the world ticket and plan a 6 week itinerary taking in Hong Kong, Australia, Hawaii and The United States. I remember counting down the days until we were due to depart from Heathrow for Hong Kong at the end of July 1994. I've always found travelling a great way to broaden my outlook on life and see through challenges to potential solutions. I knew that I couldn't go back to the same old life. As we were spending the final day of the trip in Boston, I found myself in the most wonderful bookshop there. A large yellow volume caught my eye whilst browsing the personal development shelves. It was titled "Zen & The Art Of Making A Living" By Laurence Boldt. If you decide to purchase the book, please be warned that it's a weighty tome and takes the reader through a series of structured thinking processes with the aim of helping you find the work you were born to do.

I began to work through the book on the overnight flight back from Boston to London and was so gripped by the process that I stayed awake virtually all night. The vocation that popped out of the other edge of the sausage machine was psychologist. I can recall the moment when the idea of retraining as a psychologist first occurred to me. There was an exercise in the book that encouraged me to think about the subjects I'd studied up to now and what I'd most enjoyed. I loved the psychology courses I'd studied at Liverpool in the early 1980s but had never been able to see how I could carve out a career as a psychologist. More than 10 years after finishing my first degree, I'd acquired some valuable business and consulting experience, especially of individuals and organisations going through major change. It was the matching of organisational change to psychology that created the spark of an idea to become an organisational psychologist. Everything starts with an idea and 10 years and 2 degrees after reading "Zen & The Art Of Making A Living", I proudly qualified as a chartered psychologist with the British Psychological Society in early 2005.

So I was already a qualified psychologist before life went into sharp decline and I ended up in hospital in 2006. You might think I should have known better by this stage. Looking back, I feel as though the 10 years training to become chartered was just the academic piece of the jigsaw puzzle. The practical component came in the following 5 years and what I learned in that period seems far more valuable in many ways, which is why I wanted to create this book.

What does this mean for you and finding the purpose of your life? A few things spring to mind. Firstly, life has an uncanny habit of giving us what we ultimately need, not necessarily what we want at any given moment. So it's important to be open to the messages and learning that come from challenges and difficulties. When we come to believe that there are no mistakes and wrong decisions, only learning and growth, then life does genuinely feel happier and more purposeful. Secondly, interesting mental connections and ideas tend to occur when the mind is relaxed and not deliberately trying hard to solve the thorny problem of "where on earth is my career heading?" Somehow, I attracted "Zen & The Art Of Making A Living" into my life at just the moment when I was calmly receptive to the messages it contained. Thirdly, be open to making connections between episodes of life which have been deeply enjoyable and where you have been "in flow". In other words where time seems to just stand still because you become lost in the process what you are doing, for its own sake. I feel that these moments provide the biggest possible clues to finding your life purpose in work. Ask yourself the questions "when has time seemed to stand still for you and what were you doing"?

There's a saying I like that goes along the lines of "when the why is compelling enough, the how becomes easy". Finding your purpose is the ultimate "why". At the highest level, our life purpose is to love and be loved according to Deepak Chopra. There's something to meditate on….

Chapter 12 – Cherish Your Connections For A Balanced Life

"Ultimately, the reason why love and compassion bring the greatest happiness is simply that our nature cherishes them above all else"
The 14th Dalai Lama

At The University Of Rock Bottom

There are times in life when we realise the true value of friendship and the spring of 2006 was one of those times for me. Many people would have been highly embarrassed at the thought of even setting foot inside a psychiatric hospital but not my friend Tim. I first met Tim in early 1995 when I decided to take voluntary redundancy from my job as a project manager at Mercury Communications in Milton Keynes. Tim was allocated as my outplacement consultant whose role was to help me find a new job and in this case, a whole new career. Tim certainly did that and a whole lot more. From the moment we met, there was a glint in Tim's eye and we got on like the proverbial house on fire. I immediately loved Tim's deep spiritual thinking and worldly wisdom, honed over many years spent in the Royal Marines and as a career counselor. We'd find ourselves locked in timeless and fascinating conversations for hours. Such was my admiration for Tim that I asked Tim and his wife Kim to become Godparents to my first son James, born in August 1996.

Recently, Tim shared how he felt on seeing me timid and completely withdrawn in the corner of my hospital room in April 2006. He said it was like seeing someone he didn't know. The strange thing is when I think back to that time now, it also feels like I'm recalling someone else's life, rather than my own. The healing has been profound and I have a sense of gratitude about the gift in the experience and how it has helped me to become a more understanding and loving person.

When a true friend shows love and concern when you are at rock bottom, it's something you never forget. I've learned to cherish the connections I have with special friends because of the way they stood by me. True happiness is found in connecting with others and especially in sharing moments of joy with others whom we really care about. Relationships seem to magnify the whole human experience and can make the highs higher as well as the lows lower, so it's important we give conscious thought to who we develop significant connections with.

Caring For The Happiness Of Others

The title of my earlier book "The Purpose Of Life Is Happiness" was inspired by the words of the 14th Dalai Lama. Perhaps one of the reasons why falling in love generates such happy feelings for us is that we find ourselves genuinely care for the happiness of another in a profound way. Caring for the happiness of others may also help to explain why highly successful entrepreneurs can become philanthropists, giving away enormous fortunes in the process. It's also why performing random acts of kindness can be so fulfilling.

Many business leaders reach a point where their work seems to have less real meaning and there is a deep yearning for something more significant. While this may be the result of a "mid-life" re-evaluation as described in the previous chapter, a frequent desire is to want to give back, to contribute in some way towards the happiness of others and potentially leave a legacy in the world

Random Acts Of Kindness

Performing random acts of kindness and making a difference to a stranger's life without wanting to be acknowledged or appreciated tend to make us feel happy and less stressed. Why is that? I think it links back to The Dalai Lama's ideas on compassion. We all have an inbuilt need for love. We can't give what we don't have and by performing random acts of kindness, we are proving to ourselves that we are loved and cared for. Perhaps this is why it feels so good.

Remove The Two Greatest Hindrances To Compassion – Anger & Hatred

We almost know instinctively soon after meeting someone who is holding onto anger or hatred. Both are highly unattractive emotions which inhibit feelings of love and compassion. I've discussed the power of true forgiveness earlier – it really works!

Stop Trying To Be Like Your Parents

Being a parent is one of the toughest yet most rewarding things many of us will ever take on. You have to make it up as you go along and all most of us can really do is to parent in similar fashion to the way we were parented. For most of my childhood and even early adulthood, I very much wanted to be like my Dad – extremely academic and highly successful in business. Gaining a scholarship to Oxford seemed like a tough act to follow and it wasn't until I gained three University degrees that I subconsciously gave up the chase.

We all have different skills and talents, yet it can be easy to fall into the trap of thinking that we need to live up to attributes, skills or talents that our parents may have possessed. I did and all that happened was I became unhappy and unfulfilled in early adulthood. Finding my passion and purpose was the thing that really enabled me to become my own person and let go of the need to emulate my Dad. Once that happened, I felt free and genuinely happy in my own skin. The world we inhabit now is very different from that of our parents at a similar age. This is why I feel that the best thing we can ever do for our children is teach them to be independent and follow their own life purpose.

Social Media Connections Aren't Enough

The nature of contact and friendships has definitely changed with the advent of social media sites such as Facebook and Twitter. While it's great to connect with friends in this way to share updates, photos and videos, the experience doesn't come anywhere near the sense of connection we have when meeting or even speaking on the 'phone.

We can learn a huge amount about how to deal with stress and how to be create a healthy work life balance by looking at depression and how to be depressed. When I was depressed, the last thing I wanted to do was connect with anyone else and that just added to the sense of isolation and depression, so the whole thing becomes a vicious circle. To be happy, we need to share ourselves, our love, our friendship and our time with those we care about and who care about us.

Chapter 13 – Don't Worry, Be Happy

"More Than Half Of Our Hospital Beds Are Occupied By People With Nervous And Emotional Troubles."
Dale Carnegie, author of "How To Stop Worrying And Start Living".

Why Worry?

Everything we do is because we believe it will take us away from pain or towards pleasure and that in some way we will feel better as a result. If you have a small problem to solve, a little focused thinking can often come up with a solution. Implement the solution and you're done; problem solved and worry over. The challenge comes when the problem is too large and complex to be solved in this simple way. Using the same method results in "rumination", described earlier.

The Worry Habit & How It Starts

Worry can be an easily formed habit and it certainly was for me. Dipping back into childhood for a few moments, I can recall worrying that I'd not done any piano practice when taking weekly music lessons as a 10 year old. I dreaded going to school on Fridays and would do virtually anything to get out of attending my 11.15am piano lesson. Rather than the obvious solution of doing a few minutes piano practice each evening, I chose to focus on the problem. The problem was I didn't like my piano teacher and worried that she would be unhappy with me. Although I had some musical aptitude, it was as though I was subconsciously sabotaging this. I know this is a relatively trivial example, but I believe that when we practice worry and it becomes established in the early years of life, worry can be a particularly challenging habit to break. It's easy for worry to become a pattern which is simply repeated without conscious awareness. Unfortunately, it's also a pattern that can have serious consequences in terms of stress levels and if overindulged can potentially lead to chronic depression and anxiety.

Stop for a moment and think about a situation or situations from your own childhood when you learned to worry. None of us were born with the worry habit – we learned to "do it". Some of us learned it from our parents.

My Mum was a bit of a worrier, so worry was to some extent modeled in my upbringing. It might help to explain where the worry habit started for Mum. She was born in February 1936 as the storm clouds of war were building over Europe. Mum's father, Roy Broadbent was an RAF officer in World War II who won the DSM. I should feel very proud of my maternal grandfather, though I don't to be honest. Roy Broadbent and my grandmother, Elsie King "got it together" out of wedlock; a much frowned upon predicament in those days. Mr Broadbent and his family considered my grandmother to be below their station in life and Pamela King, my mother was born and raised for the first 14 years out of wedlock. Mum told me how she moved from boarding house to boarding house as a child, changing school many times. She also lived through the hardships of the war and rationing. Perhaps it's not surprising that one of Mum's core beliefs was that life was hard. Those early years were definitely hard for her and even when my grandmother met and married a much older man, Jack Briggs soon after the war, Mum had a difficult relationship with her stepfather. She was fond of telling me how she would love to have gone to University but her stepfather wouldn't allow it and instead, she went to work in an ice-cream factory, aged 16. It makes me want to weep when I read the immaculate school reports that I still have describing Mum's model performance at Malvern Hall Grammar School for Girls in Solihull. She was a very bright and well behaved pupil with a promising future who always gave 100% effort.

Just to complete the story on my grandfather Roy Broadbent for a moment. Soon after my first son James was born in 1996, I spoke to Mum about getting in touch with her father. Mum's mum had died in 1990 and because it wasn't going to upset Elsie, Mum and I agreed that I should make contact with Mr Broadbent who we knew was still alive, telling him that he had become a great grandfather. We knew where he lived and I was able to look up Roy Broadbent in the 'phone book, knowing that he lived in a village just outside Stratford upon Avon. It was the hardest "cold call" I have ever made and my heart was literally in my mouth. An elderly lady answered the phone, prompting me to say "could I just check I have the right number please? I'd like to speak with Roy Broadbent. Does he have a sister called Lorna and a brother called Rex? The lady replied that he did and asked Mr Broadbent to come to the phone without asking me who was calling. The wait seemed to last forever and a well-spoken gentleman came to the 'phone and said "Roy Broadbent speaking".

How do you start a conversation like that? I'd not given it too much thought, believing that I probably wouldn't even get to speak to my grandfather. I said " Hello Mr Broadbent, my name is Andrew Bridgewater and my mother is called Pamela. I believe I'm your grandson". There was a long pause before the voice at the other end of the phone said "I'm sorry, I don't know what you're talking about" and hung up the receiver. I felt devastated, not just for myself but for Mum. This was the closest Mum had got to being in touch with her father for more than 50 years and the first time I had ever spoken to him. I subsequently found out that Mr Broadbent had married a lady called Ethel whom I suspect knew nothing of the existence of his illegitimate daughter (my mother). Mr Broadbent was courageous in the war but a little less so in his personal life. Mum wrote to him shortly after the 'phone conversation but there was no reply. Roy Broadbent died a few years ago, well into his nineties, shortly before Mum died at the age of 73. We know this because Mum managed to find one of the Broadbent cousins via the internet and they were able to exchange letters.

I wanted to share the detail of this part of my life story because it helps to explain why my mother might have grown up to be a worrier and believe that life was hard. I remember her telling me as a child that I shouldn't expect the best in life and then I wouldn't be disappointed. She told me many times of the sense of abandonment she felt having been estranged by her biological father. I believe that it was a lifetime of worry that killed Mum in the end. She always took great care to exercise and eat well but never conquered the worry habit. So much so that it started to annoy me after my episode of depression in 2006, because I had by then realised that worry is totally counter-productive and dangerous. Pamela Kearsley died on 1st January 2010 after two periods in intensive care brought on by a serious brain hemorrhage. Prior to the brain bleed, she was experiencing very high blood pressure, brought on by years of prolonged worry and stress. As I've said, everyone has their "crack of least resistance" and left unmanaged, prolonged worry and stress will inevitably find it.

What I'm Now Learning About Worry

I'm writing this chapter during a prolonged financial challenge which has gone on for over four years. I described earlier how more than £130,000 of money that I "invested" through a business contact in Cyprus has disappeared. 2006 vintage Andrew would have worried himself literally to death over this, but I have grown through the earlier experiences and have learned the power of focusing on the solution, as opposed to just focusing on the problem. I'd like to use this episode as a case study of how to deal with worry. In a nutshell, the challenges I've experienced have provided real-life coaching for the future. This is an empowering philosophy of life which enables me to take responsibility for whatever happens, rather than remain at the effect of it as a victim. You can do the same and could see any worry-some circumstances in your life right now as providing you with real-life coaching. All it takes is a different perspective and a small mental shift.

One of the biggest differences this time in handling a significant financial challenge versus the way I handled one in 2006 is that I'm feeling inspired in a number of areas of life. I have come to believe that worry and inspiration are mutually exclusive. You can only focus on one of them at a time. Think back to a time in your life when you felt truly inspired. Take yourself back into that time now and think back to how you felt, where you were, what you saw, heard and experienced. Were you able to experience worry? I suspect not.

Something I have learned to do which is a highly effective strategy for dealing with worry is to compartmentalise my problems. It's almost as if I can put a problem away in a box and not think about it. This is the only way that I could get out there and start to replace the investment funds I sent to Cyprus to pay my sons' school fees and to begin to replace the pension monies taken by Jarl Moe. It also created a sense that I was doing something positive and constructive, rather than dwelling on the unfairness of the situation causing me to worry.

Two Simple "Slight Edge" Habits To Eliminate Worry From Your Life

My two favourite positive habits to counteract the worry habit are daily meditation and daily gratitude. I've mentioned the power of gratitude earlier, as well as how to use meditation and am convinced that these two practices, above all others have enabled me to douse the worry habit. Unfortunately, you don't work out at the gym once and stay fit for the rest of your life. The same is true with meditation and gratitude; the benefits last for as long as you continue with the practices. I'm a total convert now and will continue to meditate and practice gratitude every day for the rest of my life.

Being grateful in this moment causes us to shift away from ego-based thinking and worry to reflect positively on all the good things, circumstances, situations and people in our lives. Stop right now and make a written list of ten things you're grateful for. When you've made the list, reflect on how you feel now verses how you felt a minute or two before you made the list. Has your state changed? Do you feel different? This is a great illustration of how we are always feeling our thinking and how the way to feel better in the moment is just to change what you're thinking about. This is not a trivial point and something that's quite profound once you grasp it.

Take Responsibility For Whatever Has Happened In Your Life

This is a tough one to accept sometimes. Whatever has happened in your life, it really helps to accept responsibility for it, rather than seek to blame other people. The problem with blaming other people is that in order for the situation to improve, the other person has to do something differently and you could be waiting a very long time for that (especially if they're dead). As a business person or entrepreneur, taking personal responsibility is something that often differentiates the highly successful from the rest. There's a profound sense of personal freedom that comes from this mental shift; it's as though you have received the keys to unlock the potential that lies in The Universe. It's also a great strategy for dealing with the worry habit and developing mental resilience.

I'm still dealing with this one after "investing" the money for my son's education and my own pension with Jarl Moe. I can sit and ruminate on how unfair the situation is or I can accept responsibility for the decision I made to send the money. After all, it was my decision and no one was holding a gun to my head at the time.

Chapter 14 – Building Self-Esteem And Self-Confidence

"Marry Yourself First !"
Ken Donaldson

"Love Yourself" Is A Key Message In This Book

"Marry Yourself First" is the title of a book by Ken Donaldson, a coach whom I first worked with in early 2006 soon before being admitted to hospital with depression. It's kind of fitting that this should be included in the last chapter. It was Ken who after valiantly attempting to coach me over the telephone with an 8 hour time difference, suggested that I was exhibiting symptoms of depression and needed to seek help quickly. By the time Ken and I got on the phone for the second fortnightly call, I was in trouble – far deeper into stress and depression than any success coach could haul me out of.

I didn't really appreciate the significance of "marrying yourself first" and when I first came across the book of the same name; it seemed a slightly odd concept. I get it now though. If you don't authentically love yourself, it's very difficult to authentically love anyone else or for anyone else's love for you to be enduring. This is probably something to do with the concept that it's impossible to give what you don't have. It also makes perfect sense when you consider what happens when a relationship ends. If you genuinely love yourself, no life circumstance or situation can take that away; no partner leaving will take that love for yourself away, however acute the pain of losing the relationship might be at the time. It also means that you're less close to the edge if a lover seems critical or short-tempered and so relationships between two people who genuinely love themselves are much more storm-resistant and likely to endure.

Back in early 2006, I didn't love myself. I had a room full of self (or should that have been shelf) development books on subjects ranging from boosting self-confidence to creating wealth and none of them seemed to be working, despite multiple readings! Perhaps that next book would be the elusive one that would enable me to engineer the breakthrough – whatever I was looking for. It's so easy to focus on our faults and shortcomings in life, yet a "glass half-empty" mindset such as I had back then just leads to a life chasing happiness when happiness is infinite and surrounds us continually

What's This Got To Do With Business?

Quite a lot actually. As I mentioned earlier, positive self-regard has been identified by psychologists as the most important underlying component of emotional intelligence (EI). Emotional intelligence has gained a great deal of credibility in recent years after the publication of Daniel Goleman's book of the same name in 1995. Simply defined, emotional intelligence is the ability to handle the emotional ups and especially the downs of life and work. It's become a key factor in developing effective leadership skills and one that differentiates the best from the rest. Therefore, it's well worth investing some time and effort in developing a more positive sense of self-regard using the techniques covered in this book. Not least because it will help you deal much more effectively with stress and support a healthy work life balance.

Good Things Can Be Woven From All The Experiences Of Life

It's impossible to experience happiness without having experienced its reciprocal, just as there can be no sunrise without darkness. The key is to be able to recognise the value in stress caused by setbacks and challenges because it's here that the seeds of happiness are sown.

This is great news because with a small shift in mindset and a little practice, we can choose what to do with every life experience, good, bad and indifferent. So why not look for the positive every time? The most difficult time to do this is during or immediately after a challenge or setback, so sometimes it's just a case of getting through the emotional aftermath. This book contains plenty of practical hints and tips for doing that – meditation, gratitude and exercise for example. Sometimes we've just got to hang in there a little and the wind will change direction.

Conclusion

This book was written to help leaders like you who feel stuck and are looking for highly pertinent and practical answers to the question "how do I deal with stress and create a healthy work life balance?" I've answered the question based on what I've learned from working in business for over 30 years. By using the techniques in this book, you'll be healthier, happier, more fun to be around and much more able to prevent stress from tipping into the more sinister relatives - anxiety and depression. Prevention is so much better than cure in this area. I should know as I've tried both.

Above all, I would like to think that this book will contribute in some way to your personal wellbeing and that of the people you care most about.

I would love to connect with you personally. To enquire about booking me as a speaker or workshop facilitator or to request a personal coaching consultation, please visit :-
www.AndrewBridgewater.com or contact me by email at
Andrew@AndrewBridgewater.com

I wish you a lifetime of health and happiness; thank you for giving me the great privilege of sharing what I have learned with you.

Andrew

Bibliography And Recommended Reading

The Slight Edge: Secret To A Successful Life by Jeff Olson

The Inside Out Revolution by Michael Neill

You Can Heal Your Life by Louise Hay

Eat That Frog by Brian Tracy

The Seasons Of Life by Jim Rohn

Zen & The Art Of Making A Living by Laurence Boldt

The Depression Cure by Dr Steve Ilardi

Younger Next Year by Dr Henry Lodge & Chris Crowley

Emotional Intelligence by Daniel Goleman

Walk With The Wise by Tim Binder & Ron Owen

Portfolio People by Max Comfort

The pH Miracle by Dr Robert O Young

Marry Yourself First by Ken Donaldson

The Power of The Subconscious Mind by Joseph Murphy

17192912R00080

Printed in Great Britain
by Amazon